The
Migrants'
Child

BUD SALSBURY

LifeRich
PUBLISHING®

THE HOLY BIBLE, NEW INTERNATIONAL VERSION®, NIV® Copyright © 1973, 1978, 1984, 2011 by Biblica, Inc.® Used by permission. All rights reserved worldwide.

Scripture quotations marked (NLT) are taken from the Holy Bible, New Living Translation, copyright © 1996, 2004, 2007 by Tyndale House Foundation. Used by permission of Tyndale House Publishers, Inc., Carol Stream, Illinois 60188. All rights reserved.

LifeRich Publishing is a registered trademark of The Reader's Digest Association, Inc.

LifeRich Publishing books may be ordered through booksellers or by contacting:

LifeRich Publishing
1663 Liberty Drive
Bloomington, IN 47403
www.liferichpublishing.com
1 (888) 238-8637

Because of the dynamic nature of the Internet, any web addresses or links contained in this book may have changed since publication and may no longer be valid. The views expressed in this work are solely those of the author and do not necessarily reflect the views of the publisher, and the publisher hereby disclaims any responsibility for them.

Any people depicted in stock imagery provided by Getty Images are models, and such images are being used for illustrative purposes only. Certain stock imagery © Getty Images.

ISBN: 978-1-4897-2171-6 (sc)
ISBN: 978-1-4897-2169-3 (hc)
ISBN: 978-1-4897-2170-9 (e)

Library of Congress Control Number: 2019934160

Print information available on the last page.

LifeRich Publishing rev. date: 02/16/2019

The events in this story are true. But because the passage of time in a child's mind is difficult to gauge, some of the dates and times may not be exact. However, I have tried to be as accurate as my memory allows. I have changed the names of all people included in the book to respect their privacy and identity; except those who have given me permission to include them and their stories.

Ephesians 3: 7
"I became a servant of this gospel by the gift of God's grace given me through the working of his power."

INTRODUCTION

The Migrants' Child is a story that I originally intended to write for my wife, to share with our children and our grandchildren. I wrote it because there was a natural curiosity among them about my childhood and the circumstance of growing up in the fields during the 1940s and 1950s. There were questions my children ask that I rarely answered. Some things I did not want to remember and there were things that I was afraid to let them know.

I would like to dedicate these stories my grandchildren, Alix, Will, Jessica, Bryce, Riley, Emily, Makenna, John, Kate, Braden, Kayla, Charleigh, Sophie, and Jones, with the hope that they will grow to understand the love and grace that God has for them. And especially to my grandson Trevor who was ever so curious about my past but unfortunately will not be able to read or hear the answers I wish I would have given him.

Even today there are children who like myself grew up in the orchards and fields of California, Oregon and Washington. Always moving, changing schools, houses and friends. Going wherever their parents decide to go with no choice, but to follow, and live the life of a migrant.

I called this story "The Migrants' Child" because that is what I was. Although we did not refer to ourselves as migrants. Others referred to us by that name and other names as well. Names like transients, itinerants, field hands or gypsies. However, when asked what we did for a living we said we were laborers, field hands or fruit pickers. But to a large portion of our society the term migrant workers seemed appropriate. This term was taken from the depression era and it seems to describe our life adequately.

Every family has a story, there are things they share and things that are kept under wraps for years and perhaps forever. These are things that you just can't share with classmates or teachers. Things that take place behind closed doors that you are not comfortable sharing with anyone else, so you keep quiet and pretend that everything is normal. My family was not so different in that respect but I have decided to put on paper some of the things as I remember them.

During our life together my wife Carol has coerced me several times to tell friends and family about parts of my childhood and how I grew up. Normally I refuse to talk about it. But, on occasion with the right group of friends I have revealed some of the incidents that have had an impact on my life. I try to bring out the humor in a story whenever possible. But somethings just aren't funny. I have never told anyone all of my story, and I have never attempted to write about it before. However, with my wife's encouragement I am attempting to put on paper some events of my life. I realize that if my stories are ever going to be recorded I should just do it. As a friend of my often says "if not now when".

I will attempt to capture my life in short clips. Attempting to encompass a certain place or an age. As stated my original intention was to do this just for the children. However, my wife and some friends have pointed out that perhaps someone other than family will glean something positive from this story. So that is my hope and my only reason for making my story available to others outside my family.

My story is not all that different from a lot of other children who grew up in similar social or economic conditions. In fact I can think of several neighbors and playmates who probably had it worse than I did during their lives. I will write of the times and events that are memorable to me, and like so many others who reminisce, we recall the very best and the very worst of times. I want to point out that since this is my story it is from my memory. Others who may have been involved can have a different memory of the events but this is the way I remember it. I have tried very hard to be as accurate as possible. And to the best of my knowledge everything written is true.

I don't in any way want the reader to feel that all of my memories were of hard times. But things were certainly rough. Money was scarce and living conditions weren't always the best. It's these things that make my childhood stand out as different from other children. These events have had a very large impact on who I am today and any success I may have had along the way. The violence of my childhood, the poverty and the insecurity brought about with the constant moving from one place to the next to follow the harvest, all play a role in who I am.

As consumers we eat the fruit and vegetables that show up in the stores but give little or no thought as to how they came to be there. How do they get from the orchards or fields? Who are the people who harvest the produce for us? And how do these people live? Can they make a living, how much are they paid? It is this migrant life and the individuals who lived that life that has captured the interest of the people who have heard some of my stories. However, that is only a part of what I am about to write. I'm also going to include the times in my life that only a loving God could have gotten me through. These are the things that are most important. Amazingly the grace of God is there even for the child of a migrant.

If you learn even one thing from my story I hope it is the message that no matter what the circumstances, you don't have to be a victim of your environment. You are never alone! **God has a plan for all of our lives; be still and listen.** There is always someone else worse off than you. If you lose an eye think of the blind person who would trade almost all he owns for one good eye in a second. If you lost a leg what about the man who has no legs or no arms. All of us are so caught up in our own dilemma. We don't always choose to take the time to look at those around us, those that are facing problems that we can't imagine. As a teenager I was no different. I couldn't quite grasp why God had singled me out to pick on. Why did other people have families that were normal and I was stuck in this awful situation, embarrassed and feeling that I was not as good as those who had parents and always wondering what I did to make mine leave me with someone else.

If I were to give this story a theme it would probably be "Why Me" "what did I do to deserve this ". As this story goes forward perhaps you will understand that this is not an appeal for sympathy, no way am I trying to convey a "woe is me" story. To the contrary it is no more than the natural wonderings of any child in similar circumstances. A story of hope, anger and above all else forgiveness and transformation.

My life, similar to the lives of most people can be split into parts discernable by an age, a location or an event. I have decided to split mine into several distinct parts. "Early Childhood" "Transformation" "Teenage Years" and then into adulthood. "Why Me" is a question that is meant to be asked in two completely different ways. Sometimes as a child I would ask with tears of sadness in my eyes, feeling ashamed and embarrassed about my life with my grandparents. Then later as I entered into adulthood I could ask the same question with a smile and tears of joy streaming down my cheeks when I ask God why me? How could I be so fortunate; how could you love me so much after all I have done. In the middle of these times during my adolescence there were no tears but I still asked the question. I just wasn't allowed to cry; even during times when it would have been normal for most children or even adults to cry due to some event or circumstance. However, for me during that time in my life the tears ceased. I was far too hardened and too bitter to show emotion of any kind.

There were places in my life that were very violent. I won't attempt to recall or tell of all the violence witnessed by my brother and me simply because it's not necessary. I hope the reader will just accept that those acts of violence which I chose to describe were repeated on numerous occasions throughout our lives. Same act, different time, different city, different day, violence remains the same. However, those that I have included I feel will help the reader to understand how I lived and what it was like. Some of the things I witnessed or endured were the things that I believe helped contribute to who I became. At times I will attempt to let you know how I felt about events and circumstance as they occurred in my life. However, as my family well knows I'm not very good at expressing my feelings. But, for this story, I am determined to suppress that part of my personality and try to the best of my ability to let you know how it felt to be "The Migrants' Child".

As stated earlier we were a family of migrant workers. All of us. That is what we did to make a living. My biological mom, her boyfriend, grandma, grandpa and my uncle Richard, his wife, my two brothers and I were what comprised the family. Each of us following the crops and fields of almost anything that could be grown, cultivated or harvested. We picked grapes, cotton, peaches, pears, apples, almonds, walnuts, cherries, nectarines, apricots, prunes, carrots and others crops as well. Even at a young age I was required to work the fields during harvest, just as I did picking cotton at age 5. I could help with the harvest of grapes that were used to make raisins as well.

Normally these were cut off the vine with a very sharp knife and then laid out on a very large canvas in the sun. There the grapes would dry or dehydrate and then they were raisins. I imagine that technology today would have them run through some form of dehydrator both for efficiency and hygiene. Plums that were used for making prunes was another crop that I was able to assist in harvesting at a very young age. When the plums were ripe a large canvas was stretched under the tree and an adult would climb around the tree and pound on the limbs with a large mallet knocking the plums as well as any bat that may be sleeping in the tree to the canvas below. My brother Clancy and I would then crawl around on our hands and knees and pick up the fallen fruit. The same technique was also used to pick walnuts and almonds. Modern equipment and technology has placed attachments on the front of tractors and now the whole tree is shaken at one time. Again this is far more efficient than the way it was done in the 1940s and 1950s. We worked side by side with Mexicans, Blacks, and a large population of under educated whites from around the United States. The majority of the workers that weren't Mexican came from the Deep South. These were people who had migrated west to make a living when there was no other work available. All people from different backgrounds working together with a common goal. Trying to find a job to make the money to support their families. Some sending their money home and others like us who were all together would pick up the entire family on a moment's notice and go where the money was better or the crops more abundant. In essence willing to do anything to earn a buck when jobs and money were scarce.

A MESSAGE TO MY FAMILY

It's important that each of my family members reading this understand that I am writing this primarily for them, although others may have the opportunity read it. As each person grows they are faced with lots of decisions just as I was. Each and every road you take in life will eventually come to a point where each person must go one direction or another. That is a decision that only you can make. However, with each choice you make there will be circumstances attached to that choice, some good, and some bad. Keep that in mind as you read further. I didn't always make the best choice.

When I first started to write this story I didn't intend for it to be a story about Christianity or faith. But to tell my story it is imperative that I describe several incidences in my life that only God would be able to help me through. There can be no other explanation. In fact, the more I have written about my life the more I realize that this story is primarily about Faith and Grace and not just about me. A prominent Christian author and comedian once said that until God is finished with His plans for your life; you will continue to live. Maybe that's why I am still alive today because there were times when I should have died and I didn't. Does that mean there is more in life that I haven't finished yet? I certainly hope so.

Haven't most people experienced something in their lives that makes them wonder "how did I get through that"? Why didn't I die, or why was I chosen?

In the lives of most people there is usually a place and a circumstance that is a point of awakening. A place where you decide which career path you are going to follow, who you're going to marry, and should I do the right thing or take the path most comfortable. But most of all do I believe there is a God or am I the master of my destiny? There may even be more than one place in your life that becomes a life changer for you or your family. When the road of life splits which way should you go, right or left, which way; it's your call; your circumstances and your consequences with the outcome of that decision. I can't be there to make them for you. It's these decisions which make the stories in our lives. Those are the stories that shape each of us into who we are. I had to make my choices and it wasn't always the right one. I truly regret some of the decisions I made, but once they're made it's difficult to change them, and if you do, there will be another fork, another road and another circumstance to face. While those things shape us; they also help us become stronger. And if we will let it happen, if we will be still and listen we may also become closer to the God who has helped us through those times even though we may not know it. That's the good message "if you will just listen God has a plan for your life" and it is a far better plan than the one you have.

That being said I will continue with "The Migrants' Child".

THE MIGRANTS' CHILD

Every story must have a beginning, an ending and a cast of characters. I have read the work of some authors who may take chapters to introduce the characters in their stories. In my story I will begin with the cast of characters. There aren't very many so it is only a couple of paragraphs. These are the people you will need to know to understand the beginning of my life and why it starts as it does.

THE CAST

John Lee Salsbury: my grandfather. He will always be referred to as Pop or Dad because that is what I called him and he was the only Dad I ever knew. Sometimes I would call him daddy, a name I would use when I was getting a whipping and I would cry out "no daddy don't hit me again, I won't do it any more". And also like every little boy if I wanted something I would say please daddy. Pop was born in Meacham Oregon in 1903. His parents John Samuel Salsbury and Julia Armenta Graves came across the trail from Missouri to Oregon in a wagon train. For some reason known only to him he claimed Armenta to be from the Yakima Indian Tribe. After researching the genealogy to the best of my knowledge she was not. I sometimes wonder if he did that so we could have something to set us apart from the "normal families". I know I professed to be part Indian for a good part of my life and into adulthood and I was proud of it.

Pop moved to Yakima and spoke of traveling from Meacham to Yakima in a horse drawn wagon. His Dad was a logger and died in Yakima at a very early age. Julia remarried shortly after the death of her first husband. She married Richard Bashan. They had only one child that I am aware of also named Richard. Pop's step father had little use for education and believed that as soon as a boy was able, he should work and help support the family. He also believed that whipping a son would make him a stronger man. Pop stayed with his mom and step dad until age twelve. At twelve years old he was in the third grade. I can't fathom what it must have been like to be 12 and a third grader. Most kids are in the 6th or 7th grade by that age. Dad had the intelligence, but he was never given the opportunity to attend school on a regular basis. That same year he decided to run away from home. As a mere 12 year old, Dad left home and went to an area called Horse Heaven in the Lower Yakima Valley. There he was a sheep herder living in a wagon and camping under the stars every night. At the end of summer the sheep would be returned to their winter fields thus ending his summer employment. To the best of my knowledge he never returned to live at home again and had no further contact with his step dad. I have always marveled at that story. First because he was 12 and a third grader and second because he was apparently capable of leaving home at such an early age and managed to care for himself from that point forward. Dad was a pretty small person by almost any standard, 5ft. 5inches tall. For some he had a nickname (Shorty) but there were only a very few people in the world that could call him Shorty. If you weren't one of those few he would warn you once. However, if you used that term again he would hit you before you finished the sentence. He really didn't have a temper, but he felt that no one was going to make fun of him. He believed Shorty used by most folks was a derogatory name that was making fun of his size and that just wasn't going to be tolerated.

Rose Zacharias Salsbury: Born 1906 in Milton-Freewater, Oregon. Rose is always referred to as Mom by my brother and me. Rose was one of about 23 children in the Zacharias clan. There is not a lot to say about Mom at this point other than she was by all standards a very large, very strong lady and she had a terrible temper. Mom had an 8th grade education that she was very proud of. She married John in about 1923 and had two children. Richard Otto and Evelyn Armenta (my birth mother). As I progress through this story; anytime I say that Mom told me; or Mom said; those events need to be taken lightly. While there may be an element of truth in the things she has told me, there is also a tendency to stretch that element to her advantage.

Evelyn Armenta Salsbury: Evelyn will not be referred to as Mom but simply Evelyn throughout this story. I will always use her name rather than calling her Mom because as children growing up that's the only reference to her we ever had. My brothers and I never knew her and were never told anything about her that would not be considered derogatory. I am aware that Evelyn gave birth to five sons from at least four fathers.

Clarence Lee Phillips (Clancy) Clancy was Evelyn's first child. Evelyn was only fifteen when Clarence Lee (Clancy) was born. The father was twenty one and they were married at some point before the birth of her first child. During the next four years Evelyn had divorced Phillips and married Wallace La Rue. She left Wallace but did not divorce him and met Charles Elmer Rickman in March or April of 1946. Evelyn was living with Rickman when her second son was born in August of that year.

Charles Richard Rickman: (Buddy) aka: Bud Richard Salsbury was born in Delano California. Rickman supposedly said. "If I have to pay the bills he is going to have my name". "Even if he's not mine". I can't attest to the absolute accuracy of that story but it is what we were told. I was also told by Mom and Dad that I was born with my right foot pointing out at a right angle and bent so I would have had to walk on the inside of my foot rather than on the bottom of it. Mom always said my foot was deformed because Evelyn insisted on wearing a girdle so she would look attractive and not fat when she was pregnant. I have no idea if that could be true or not. I wore boots when I was little and Mom took credit for straightening my foot by massaging and twisting it each day while rubbing it with hot oil and bending it to straighten it out. As I said I don't know how much of that is accurate but my right foot does point very slightly to the right, not straight ahead. However, it is so minimal that it was never an issue of any kind as I matured, walked, ran or played ball.

I went to the hospital in Bakersfield Ca. soon after my birth and received all the usual things that they do to babies. Rickman must have paid the bill because my birth certificate does indeed say Charles Richard Rickman, of Delano California. No one but Evelyn ever knew who my biological father was, and she would never tell. Perhaps it was Wallace La Rue or someone who was totally unknown to the family, and maybe she didn't actually know. I'll never find out. However, it was not Rickman, he was away in the Navy when I was conceived and did not meet Evelyn until she was in her third month. Evelyn later gave birth to Rickman's true biological son.

Lincoln Levi Rickman (Buzzy) born in October 1947. Evelyn's other two sons Wallace and Robert Bunton were born later and are not a part of this story and I know nothing of their childhoods. However, I may speak of them briefly at some point as adults. But, for now just focus on the life of the three oldest boys, Clancy, Buddy, and Buzzy.

MY STORY

Temperatures in the San Joaquin Valley in August are extremely hot. Normally it stays between 95 and 110 degrees all month. I have no reason to believe it would have been any different on August 10, 1946 the day that Charles Richard Rickman (Buddy) that's me, came into the world. I was born in a small one room cabin that was used by the migrants for housing while working on the farms during that time. By the late 1940s and into 1950s these buildings were pretty dilapidated and were more of a shack than a cabin. These dwellings were referred to as camps by those who lived in them. The workers moved from place to place following the crops, often staying in one of these cabins if it were available. However, if none were available they would stay in a tent until it was time to move on to the next field or camp, hoping to get better accommodations and better wages at the next place. These cabins or shacks normally had electricity, comprising of a bulb hanging in the middle of the room and an outlet to supply an electric burner for cooking. No running water, no inside plumbing and definitely no refrigerator or air conditioning in those days. We didn't live in a little white house with a picket fence and a grass yard in which to play. That was all fairy tales for the people who lived in the camps. A dream that would probably never come true for most of the people living there. The cabins I remember were either white or weathered wood. The walls were ¾"boards with no paint on the inside and no insulation. The floors were boards pushed together as tight as possible. There was no linoleum or anything of that nature to cover the floor just the bare wood worn smooth by the boots and soles of the people occupying the space before us. These buildings were on posts or blocks and were a couple of feet off the ground. If you looked down you could see the ground through the holes in the floor. During the heat of the day children would crawl under the house for the shade and coolness. There was no grass so children played marbles, hide and seek, kick the can or Mumblety-Peg in the bare ground around the camp. Mumblety-Peg was played between two people with a knife. Each stood opposite the other with our feet shoulder-width apart. The first person then took the knife and threw it to "stick" in the ground as near to the middle between the opponent's feet as possible. That person would then move their foot to the knife thereby decreasing the distance between their feet. The second person would repeat the process. The distance between our feet would become narrower and narrower the skill and courage of the players would determine the outcome. If a player stuck the knife in his opponent's foot he lost by default, but also because we had to quit and stop the bleeding. This did happened from time to time but not that often. This game combined your courage and your ability to throw a knife. As children (little boys) we thought it was great fun. If you stuck your opponent's foot not only would you lose but you may possibly get your butt kicked depending on who was the bigger and toughest of the two.

Bathrooms in these camps were outhouses shared by everyone. There were no showers so bathing was done on Saturdays in a # 10 wash tub (a large round galvanized tub) in the middle of the room, or with just a wash cloth and a pan. For the kids bathing was done in the closest irrigation canal. We would grab a bar of soap proclaiming we were going to bathe but all the while knowing it was a good excuse to just go swimming (if you knew how to swim). Some places had a common laundry area and a hose was usually available which we sometimes used to wash off or bathe. Staying cool at night meant either running a fan, sleeping on top of the blankets, or wearing as little as possible; usually all three. It was in one of these cabins that I was born. If you look at my birth certificate the place of birth is Delano, California. I do not believe that Delano in 1946 had a hospital, doctor, nurse or any type of building suitable for medical facilities. I was told Delano was a very small town at that time. It was comprised of a few businesses, a movie theater, a station that also served as the local store, a post office building of sorts, and a bar where everyone could go on Saturday night and spend a week's wages. Which is exactly what my family did.

As I said we were migrant workers following whatever farm crop that would pay a day's wage for our labor. It was not an easy life. I'm not sure if we had to pay rent for the cabins we stayed in, but probably so. They were usually in a grouping of six or eight buildings about twenty to thirty feet apart in a small area adjacent to the farm. Occasionally these buildings were on the land of the farmer and I presume they were owned by him. Frequently the farm or farmer that these camps supported was included in the name of the place. Such as "Peterson's Camp" or "Musser's Camp" or any other name describing a location. Those that were equipped with a wash area almost always had a large cement tub. You could wash out a load of clothes using a scrub board then wring them out by hand. A scrub board was a tool used by women of that era to clean the clothes, it had a corrugated surface on which they would rub the clothes up and down scrubbing them clean as they soaked them in the soapy water. After which the clothes were rinsed and then twisted by hand to wring the water from them so they would dry faster. Clothes were hung or placed over a clothes line. A clothes line was nothing more than a rope or a line strung between two buildings and shared by the occupants of the two cabins involved.

This was our community. The kids who were too young to work played together in the fields and the adults would socialize during the week, having a drink after work and informing one another of any upcoming work and how much they were paying at the next farm. If you were angry at a family for whatever the reason, or if you didn't think they worked as hard as they should you simply didn't keep them informed of where the next job was. All in all it was a simple, uncomplicated way of life.

This was typical of the houses we lived in while working as migrant. However, a large majority of them sat about 2 feet off of the ground

EARLY MEMORIES

When I was three we were living in one of those one room houses in Winters, California. Winters is located in the northern part of California and closer to the coast than the San Joaquin Valley. It gets cold there and it rains. I was told by Mom that Clancy, Buzzy and I were living there with Evelyn and Rickman. Buzzy was too little to do much by himself but Clancy and I would get up in the night and go to Mom and Pop's cabin for food and shelter. I was pretty small and I would be covered in mud or dirt from falling as we sloshed our way to their cabin. Pop would have to use the hose at the laundry area to clean me up before feeding us and putting us to bed. It was during this time that Rickman and Evelyn decided to leave Winters Ca. and go to Oklahoma. He had family there and would be able to get a job as a machinist, a trade he had learned in the Navy. They left Clancy and I with Mom and Dad and took their son Buzzy with them.

Sometime after they left us in Winters, California, Clancy age seven was walking alone down a highway at night after going to the movie by himself. He was struck by a car and suffered severe head injuries. The injuries were severe enough that he had to undergo extensive surgery and was in the hospital for a very long time. I remember seeing him in the hospital with bandages around his head. They wouldn't let me in the hospital so I stayed outside and sat on Dad's shoulders while Clancy came to the window and waved to me. I was terribly upset that my brother was hurt so bad and that I couldn't get to him. I cried so hard that it was decided that I could not go back to the hospital during the time he was there. When his injuries finally healed the Doctor said he was not allowed to be hit in the head (interpreted you can't spank Clancy any more). He had a huge scar running down the side of his head where he had been sown back together. I'm not sure if it were true but later in life we were told that all of the dirt and gravel from the road could not be removed from his injuries. I used to tease him about having rocks in his head, (not always a smart move on my part, he was bigger than I was).

When Clancy was released from the hospital Evelyn and Rickman were still in Oklahoma. Evelyn hadn't seen him since the accident. She informed Rickman she was going to take Buzzy and return to California to check on Clancy. She left while Rickman was at work and took all of her belongings with her. Probably a good indication that she did not intend to return. When she arrived in Winters she started living with Robert Bunton. Bunton was apparently not prepared for raising three boys so Clancy and I soon returned to our habit of running away in the night to Mom and Dad's place. Other than seeing my brother in the hospital my earliest memory was of a time we ran away. Clancy got me out of the bed that we shared and we left in the dark. Buzzy was too small to take with us. We were standing beside one of the white cabins and it was dark but I could still see. Clancy was looking forward around the corner of the cabin. I assume he was making sure we could make a break for it without being spotted. I looked back and saw a man coming for us. I still remember the fear I felt at that time, I remember being grabbed but I don't remember a thing of what happened after that. I only remember the fear of being caught.

Somewhere between my third and fourth birthday, spring or summer of 1950. Evelyn had obviously decided not to return to Oklahoma. She and Bunton must have decided that three boys was not what they wanted in life either. They apparently wanted a new start with no responsibilities and no kids to hold them back. I don't know all of the particulars of what transpired between Evelyn and her parents, but she and Bunton decided to leave the three of us with Mom and Dad and start a new life somewhere else. According to Mom, Evelyn came by one night handed the three of us to her and Dad and told them "I never want to see you or these boys ever again" and she left. According to Evelyn who I spoke with later in my adult life Mom and Dad took us from her and said don't try and get them back or I'll call the police. I really don't know which is the true story and it doesn't really matter. The fact remains that I was raised by Mom and Dad from that point on and Evelyn never came back into our lives or tried to contact us again.

BUZZY

Shortly after Evelyn left the three of us with her Mom and Dad, they in turn must have decided that three boys was probably more than they could handle as well. I have heard many reasons as to why one of us had to go. Why they could keep two grandchildren and walk away from one. I have considered all of the excuses that I was told over the years that would justify their decision but cannot in any way understand how or why it was done. My favorite excuse was that Buzzy was a very mean baby, and that he was trying to hurt me by hitting me with a hatchet. Mom said several times she had to take the weapon away from him. Personally I have a hard time believing a 20 month old child is going to clobber his 3 possibly 4 year old brother with a hatchet the first time they are left alone. However, it made for a good excuse for dumping one of us and then putting the blame on me. Since apparently I couldn't defend myself.

Evelyn's brother Richard was living in the same camp as we were. He said he and his wife had been caring for Buzzy and that he really wanted to take Buzzy but his wife forbid it. Therefore he couldn't get involved. Personally I have my own theory. I believe that being field workers it would have been extremely difficult to have a baby in the fields, especially if that child was not potty-trained. I can understand that the difficulty of caring for an untrained child in the fields would have been a burden, but it was done by others, and their families remained together. Workers in the fields in that area would get up

21

at 3:00 or 4:00 AM to start work during the cool part of the day and leave the children in the car or at the camp sleeping. When the children woke up there was sometimes a sandwich to eat before they would wander into the field in search of their parents. If you could work at that age you were expected to do so, and if not you would play with all of the other children. There was no adult supervision, but at the same time all adults were supervising each-others children. Spankings were handed out to any child by any adult for whatever infraction or line that may have been crossed.

On the day Buzzy went to his new family Evelyn's brother Richard said he was there behind a bar when Mom agreed to give Buzzy to a family who had no children. According to Richard it was he who handed Buzzy over to this new family. And he saw the one hundred dollars ($100.00) that changed hands between Mom and Buzzy's new family. A hundred dollars was a lot of money at that time. Probably about 2 weeks' wages. There was also a promise to never try and contact them again. If all of this is true and I believe it is, then maybe it was the money that was the deciding factor and not the hatchet for giving my little brother away. I will never know for sure the true motivation. However, I do know that for whatever the reason in less than a year, my big brother was almost killed by a car. My biological parent/parents abandon us. And my younger brother was sold for a hundred bucks by my grandparents. Not exactly a year I would forget.

We saw Buzzy one time after that when we were still children. A picture that I have included of me, him and Clancy is at his house in California. He and his family lived in a very small trailer in the northern part of California I remember that there was yellow grass and a big oak tree. I have no idea why we went to see them but we were only there for a short time; just an afternoon.

Figure 1 Left to Right, Buzzy, Clancy and Buddy (me)

At some point in my life I became aware of the fact that I would never see Buzzy or Evelyn again and I would wonder or fantasize what their lives were like or what I would do or say given the opportunity to confront them. I wondered if Buzzy was living a good life with plenty of food, clothes and a house in one town. At one time Mom said they lived in Sun Valley which I learned was a very upscale ski area so I assumed he was doing ok. I have no idea where she would have gotten that information, but it was not true.

During the years that followed we lived in various shacks in several towns, always working the fields and sometimes living in our tent. The tent was almost as good as the cabins but it had no floor, or the electricity that the cabins at least had. It was an adventure and I was too small to understand that we couldn't do any better or that most normal people didn't live that way. I guess that's the thing about being poor until you get big enough for someone to tell you you're poor, you have no idea you are. Especially if most of the people around you are living the same way. However, most of the time we lived in a shack wherever Dad could get a job.

KERMAN CALIFORNIA

I was about five years old and could have gone to Kindergarten while we lived in Kerman. However, Mom decided that the only thing I would learn at school is how to color and she could teach me that.

Dad and Mom were picking cotton somewhere close to town and we found a one room shanty in town and next door to the Gomez family. A Hispanic family that had a lot of kids but I can only remember three of them. Alberto who was my age and my very best friend, Esteban who was Clancy's age his close friend also, and Maria and she was a little older. I can't say that I remember a lot about Mr. Gomez but I do remember that momma Gomez was a great cook and always had tortillas and frijoles on the stove. We would wander in and out of each other's houses and play all day in the dirt we called a yard. When the cotton fields were ready to pick that year, Mom and Dad decided that I could go to the fields and pick (age 5) I was too small to actually pull a cotton sack. A cotton sack was about 8-10 ft. long and probably at least 3 ft. in diameter. It had a strap that went over your shoulder and workers would pick cotton and stuff it in the sack. Occasionally a worker would throw a hand full of dirt in the bag or a couple of rocks to add weight. This was done since they were paid by the pound. If a worker got caught doing something like this they were fired immediately. But to some people the risk was worth it. The sacks were drug along between the cotton rows and when they were filled to capacity they were taken to be weighed and recorded, then dumped in a big trailer (wagon). The wagon was probably 20 ft. long at least 8ft wide and 8ft tall with chicken wire sides that transported the picked cotton to the cotton gin or processing plant. Mom concocted a pillow case with a strap so that I could pick cotton. I drug that thing around the field and picked for as long as I could stay focused or until I had picked my daily quota of cotton (probably no more than two pillow case sacks). When my cotton had been turned in and weighed I was free to play with the other children. Kids in the field took great delight in climbing to the top of the wagon and diving into the mound of soft cotton. When the trailer was full the field boss or farmer would drive the tractor and trailer to the gin to be unloaded. While this tractor trailer combination was being driven down the highway children would climb all over the wagon and dive into the cotton. Think of the liability if kids did that today. When we reached the gin there was a giant tube (actually about 10 inches in diameter), but a giant to a five year old. The tube was lowered to the cotton and it would suck it up out of the trailer and into the gin. I was scared to death of that tube. I had seen a cartoon somewhere (I think it was Popeye) where Brutus or Popeye was sucked up into the cotton gin and came out all ensconced in a bale of cotton with only his arms, legs and head showing. That image stuck with me and when the big sucker came out I got as far away from it as possible. Once the trailer was empty we would ride back to the fields in the wagon.

Frequently at night in Kerman there was a jeep that would drive through the streets spraying for mosquitoes. The sprayers on the jeep created a fog so thick that you could hardly see through it. Any time it came through our neighborhood or close proximity to where we lived the smaller children would follow behind the jeep running in and out of the fog. I'm not sure what the repellent of choice was in the 1950s. But, I wonder how many people have had adverse effects later in their lives from all that must have been ingested.

For us life seemed close to normal living in Kerman. But I don't want to imply that all was happy and normal while living there either, because it wasn't.

Mom and Dad were both alcoholics. They would work hard when it was time to work. But they also drank hard when it was time to drink. Fights were not uncommon, either between them or with some other person at the bar. As I said I'm not going to describe all of the fights that transpired. However, on more than one occasions I saw Mom beat other women and even men with pool sticks, beer bottles, and once a cue ball. In that particular fight with the cue ball I watched as she beat a lady in their favorite bar with the cue ball she picked up from the pool table. I'm not sure what the other lady said but supposedly it was something about Clancy or me. This person then grabbed Mom, tore her blouse and scratched her breasts in the process. I remember clearly that Mom had this person laid out on top of the pool table bashing her in the face and head with that cue ball. There was blood flying everywhere, the ladies face and head were covered in blood her hair was wet with blood as though she had just stepped out of the shower, or that she was dying her hair red and it hadn't yet dried. Blood ran onto the table and stained the green cover just as it would have if someone had spilled a bottle of red wine over the table top. It took several men some time before they could separate the two women. Head wounds normally bleed profusely and this was no exception, there was blood everywhere. It covered their bodies, the table, and the floor as well as their clothing. Mom was also covered in blood but most of it belonged to the other person and it was not hers. Maybe the reason I remember this so vividly other than because of the all of the blood and the violence of the fight is that after the fight ended Mom kept saying over and over "she tore my blouse". You don't forget a fight like that, when your only five years old and it's your Mom fighting. Fighting takes on a whole new perspective when it's your parent that's fighting. That early in my life I didn't like the sight of blood. Maybe I had seen too much of it. So yes this fight left a definite impression on my memory. Throughout the years to follow, Mom got in several fights with other people; picking up whatever she could get her hands on as a weapon. Once a pool stick, another time a beer bottle and once even an oil bottle at the gas pump. She hit a man over the head with that bottle and he went down quick and hard. However, none of the fights that I recall involving her were as bad or as bloody as the incident with the cue ball. Perhaps all the other individuals just didn't tear her blouse. Or maybe she just didn't get quite so angry. I don't know. Often during or after Mom got into a fight with some woman, her husband or boyfriend would step in to continue the argument over whatever the issue may have been. That interference would often force Dad into the fight as well. Something that I really hated to see.

Mom and Dad also fought with each other when drinking. Fights were almost always started by Mom, never Dad, and usually over some trivial thing. I never remember him hitting her. However, on many occasions she would try her best to hit him. I remember one time very vividly when I was probably about 7. Dad was going to leave and Mom said she would stop him from leaving by pulling all the wires off the engine of the car. She lifted the hood and was bent over the fender with her head under the hood attempting to locate the wires. Dad closed the hood on her and booted her in the butt several times. As previously mentioned Mom was a big lady and he a small man. Therefore, he had to jump to get his foot that high. I know that Clancy and I were crying at the time but the image of that later in our lives has always made us laugh. It still does even to this day. Clancy or I will bring it up occasionally when we are together. We don't often reminisce about the good old days but when we do we always laugh about how high Dad had to jump to reach her butt. Enough of the fighting for now. However, I will mention one more fight that Dad was involved in later in the story. Only because it has relevance in what happened in our lives after that particular fight.

The point to be made is that this was our lives. The drinking and the fights that followed weren't always that violent, but this type of activity wasn't unusual either. We lived with it and really didn't think that much about it other than the fear that someone would be hurt while the fighting was taking place. Sure we were scared and I know I cried a lot but eventually I learned to accepted the fact that once the fight was over life went on as usual. Another beer and another week of work ahead of us. That's just the way it was.

There is a part of my childhood that I have struggled with a great deal. Like a lot of people of my age and generation a lot of things are just kept inside. I've not told my family members or others about this and hadn't intended to mention it. However, it is something that I remember well and it was suggested I put it in this story since it was all too often a part of my childhood. Until I started writing this story I had been very successful at keeping the memory and the emotional pain pretty much to myself. This was part of our childhood that always involved Mom when she had been drinking in excess. As I started to write, without noticing it the tears began to flow and I realized I was sitting at my computer crying. It's a memory from my early years. A memory that any child would have a hard time reliving. I have said before that Mom had a temper and fights were fairly common. However what I have not mentioned is that she would often get drunk and direct her anger at me as well. She would for no apparent reason decide to end her life or someone else's. That someone else was often mine. I only describe this once but each time it was always the same. It was during a time when we were living outside of Kerman. On this particular night Mom had been drinking and it was me who she directed her anger at that night. And just has Buzzy had been removed from the family by selling him; I could be removed just as easily by shooting me. No one would know I even existed. There were no records of my existence and it would be one less mouth to feed. I stared down the barrel of the rifle that was pointed at my head not knowing what to expect.

This wasn't the first time or the last time that this happened to me. It was just one of the many times that was brought about by alcohol, guilt, depression and anger. I can't say that on this particular day or any of the other days that I had done anything exceptionally wrong, but if I had, it certainly wasn't something I should have had to die for. When these things happened it was always extremely difficult to reason with her. Each time in my life that this happened I would stand still looking down the barrel of that gun always shaking and always crying afraid to move. She would threaten to end my life on that day for whatever the reason. Often Clancy only four and a half years older than I would step between me and the gun and take it from her. He and I agreed at some point that we would pack our bags and leave if that would make everyone happy. Each time Mom became like this one of us would step in and she would eventually relinquished the gun. We never had to actually pack our bags. In fact we didn't own any bags. I know that when you're looking down the muzzle of a gun you are never sure if this is the time the gun will go off. This scenario was repeated far too many times throughout our childhood with one or the other of us being the target of choice that particular day. The one who's life was worthless and was not worth sparing. We were just a burden that could easily be removed. The other favored child of that night would be the one stepping in to take the gun away. For some unknown reason she would never relinquish it to Dad. During the next 2-3 years I have no idea how many times I took the gun from her or how many times I was the one looking down the barrel. We didn't keep track. Clancy and I had no idea where two little boys were going to go if we were to pack our bags and leave, but we used that threat more than once to calm the situation and regain control of the gun. While this was certainly not the normal every Saturday night activity it did happen and it happened all too often. Even once in a child's life would be too often. Fortunately for all of us Mom obviously never once pulled the trigger on that old rifle that we had. When I look back I can be glad that she never picked up the 12 gage shotgun Dad owned. That thing had a hair trigger and she actually might have shot someone. I'm not sure anyone can actually put on paper the feelings that a child has when the adult that is tasked with caring for them points a gun at them and threatens to shoot telling them that they are an unnecessary burden in their life. Or that they are worthless and no one wants them. Words like that hurt. I can say for certain that I was still at an age to cry and I did a lot of that, wondering why me, what have I done that was so bad that I deserve this. Why don't I have someone who loves me? Am I not worth loving? Looking back I can't imagine what kind of demons she was dealing with or what terrible dark things may have happened in her childhood, or her past to make her do the things she did. I am not excusing her actions, or making excuses for her behavior because there are none. I've often ask myself how could the very hands that have fed and clothed you, nursed you when you were sick, comforted you when you hurt, the same one who has the responsibility to care for you; how could that person put you in a position where you have no idea if you are going to live or die at those same hands. How could those same hands that cared for me sell my brother? Or was it real that no one loved me and that I was a burden. When this was happening I was young and at the time had no real concept of death but I do know I was scared and confused. As I grew older into my teenage years there were times when Mom would do something similar but she didn't threaten me. She normally only threatened herself. I got to the point I simply said ok go ahead and I would walk out the door and leave her alone. I knew other children who had it worse than I did. One neighbor kid took off running away from his Dad dodging between the trees while his father actually pulled the trigger trying to shoot him. Fortunately he was either a bad shot or too drunk to shoot. This particular incident occurred because he was trying to stop his Dad from beating up his Mom. I knew girls who were molested by their fathers, their brothers and other relatives as well. I think that had to be worse than the whippings and mental cruelty that I endured.

For the next year or so we lived in or around Kerman, traveling occasionally to other areas depending on the crop. Mom and Dad loved to go to the stock car races where they could meet with friends have a beer and watch the cars go around in circles, always betting on the yellow one. Clancy and I would wander the stands watch the cars going around in circles and drink sodas. There were times after work Dad would take us fishing. We would fish in whatever river, lake or pond was nearby. These were happy times. We caught, perch, bluegill, catfish, crappie and bass. Perch, bluegill and crappie being our favorite but with catfish a very close second. I used a willow stick with a line and a bobber attached, and with that simple arrangement I caught an awful lot of fish. Summers were always more fun for me because Clancy was out of school and we could play together. I imagine he got tired of always having to take me with him everywhere he and his friends went, but it was good for me and I enjoyed the challenge of playing with older children. I believe being with the older children certainly had an impact and set the stage for my abilities in sports and other areas later during my school years.

THE YEAR OF MY FIFTH CHRISTMAS

On this Christmas we were living in Kerman California and were often left alone in the car outside the bars for long periods of time. We (my brother Clancy and I) spent hours sitting in the car entertaining each other playing "I Spy" or "Guess a Number" or just making up stories and games to pass the time.

My brother Clancy is four and a half years older than I am, and like older brothers everywhere, he took great pleasure in proving his superiority with a few punches, kicks, or a well-placed slap on the back of the head. After all I was the little brother and big brothers have been whipping on little brothers since Cain and Abel. He was stronger, more devious and by far meaner than I was. I still carry the memories of my older brother beating me up whenever he wished, for whatever trivial excuse he could dream up. He rarely left marks and it would anger him intensely if I refused to cry. I used that to my advantage whenever I could. Often I would wait for hours until our grandparents were back in the car, then I would cry; real tears and all "Clancy beat me up" I would wail. Then I would cry again on the rare occasions that he got a whipping for hitting me. I felt bad that he was getting whipped and I knew that I would get beat up again when he got me under the covers later or the next time we were left alone. But, to his credit no one else was allowed to beat me up. I was his little brother to beat up and his little brother to protect at the same time; just as he had those times he took the gun from Mom. He maintained that commitment to protect me but continued to harass me until our teenage years when I finally caught him on the side of the head with a lucky punch. After that he no longer beat me up. However, he would still not allow anyone else to harm me either.

Occasionally my brother and I would wander the town of Kerman where we would visit with the man who had no arms. He sat on newspapers on the sidewalk leaning against the building selling pencils for a nickel which he could do with his feet. We often crossed the street and played in the park or the town square. There we tried in vain to climb the date palm trees and knock down the dates to eat.

Sometimes we visited the man who owned the pawn shop on the square. He let us wandered through the aisles looking at all the neat stuff that we wished we could buy. I don't remember his name but he always had a sucker or piece of candy for us and never seemed in a hurry to make us leave. Perhaps he was as lonely as we were or maybe he just liked children. I'll never know. One late afternoon we came to his shop as we often did only to find that our friend the shop owner was dead. He had been tied to a chair and had been murdered. I have no idea if they found the persons involved but as I grew older I assumed it was a robbery of some sort and until recently had forgotten all about it. I suppose it is possible that I may have blocked that image from my memory as well. These are just a few of the things that I remember about this town as well as my first Christmas memory.

Kerman was and probably still is a small rural farm town in central California. It was just one of those towns that we would live in for a short period of time and it just happen to be during Christmas this particular year. Often we would move from one place to the next. Frequently during the middle of the night to wherever there were crops to be picked or weeds to be hoed, or any type of manual labor that was considered an honest day's work. However, this time we had been in Kerman longer than most of the places we had lived.

As a migrant worker and an alcoholic it meant you worked all week got paid on Saturday at noon and would be broke by Monday in time to do it all over again. Pop was a hard worker. Everything he did, he did with an intensity and determination to do his best. He strived hard to do every task correctly giving the field boss his money's worth. He used to tell me as a teenager "don't ever back up to get your pay check".

On one particular evening Mom and pop had just gone into their favorite bar for that proverbial "one beer" and a few hours later they came out with our usual soda, hamburger and chips with the promise to return shortly. Shortly usually meant you might as well settle in for a long evening of entertaining one another.

Clancy had just learned to snap his fingers and he decided we should have a contest, to see which of us could make the loudest noise. I screamed to the top of my lungs and he snapped his fingers a couple of times. We both knew who won but the outcome was predetermined. I eventually gave in and agreed that his snapping fingers was the loudest of all noises and thereby I skirted further slaps, punches and pokes from my brother.

I mention these clips from our life to help the reader understand that events in one person's life may seem strange to others. However, to the kid who knows no other life it's just another day in their life. And so it was at that Christmas at that same bar in that same year. The year of my fifth Christmas.

The thing about bars in 1951 California, as well as it is today, is that they never took a holiday. So on Christmas Eve 1951 the local bar was open for business.

Clancy and I were told that all of the usual customers, and their friends most of which we called uncle or aunt just because they were older and as such commanded a certain degree of respect, wanted to watch us get our Christmas gift. Prior to this Christmas I don't ever even remember getting a Christmas gift. However, I am sure we probably did. So the plan was that we would all go to the club for a while on Christmas Eve. There were no Christmas traditions at our house during that time in our lives. There were no memories of Christmas carols being sung, or of Pop putting a star on a tree. In fact I don't remember having a tree until I was probably 9 or 10 years old. We never shared a great Christmas dinner with family and friends as most families do. It was just us, money was always tight, and if the bar didn't open till 4:00 pm we could just hang out and play until it did. Christmas gifts in our house were not from Santa (we were taught Santa was a fake from a very early age) all Christmas presents came from our grandparents. So going to the bar on Christmas Eve would be considered a normal evening for us.

I don't quite know what the appointed time was or how it was to be determined but at a certain time when their friends had all gathered, we were taken from the car and led into the alley behind the club. Everyone found a spot and were all waiting to see the excitement of two kids getting a Christmas gift, in an alley, behind a bar. When I walked through the door into the alley I was ecstatic to see a 20 inch Murray bicycle sitting beside a car. I knew it had to be mine because I didn't own a bike and until this moment I was considered too little to ride one. My Murray had hand grips, a kick stand, and training wheels and it was red. Just exactly what every 5 year old wanted. But there was only one bike. I remember seeing Clancy looking at my bike, the only bike there, and I thought he would break into tears. I loved my brother, after all we were all each other had. And I felt terrible that there was nothing there for him. Had I been older I'm sure I would have said "take mine" I don't know how to ride anyway, but before that happened he was led to the other side of the car where there was another Murray bike; but not a new one. Clancy had received a used bike for Christmas. We were told the store only had one new bike in my size and had this very nice affordable used bike in his size. I never gave it another thought. We both had bikes and now we could ride together. It wasn't until years later that I realized the reality of Clancy not getting a new bike may have gone deeper than I was aware of at the time. His revenge for not getting a new bike was forthcoming and he did get even with me (as though it were my fault) in his own very subtle way.

Clancy was told he would have to teach me to ride my bike, and so he did. Once he had taught me how to stay upright we removed the training wheels and I was able to stay on board most of the time. I accomplished this by singing. I discovered that as long as I was singing, I didn't think about riding and I could stay upright most of the time. My favorite song "Happy Trails to you" a theme song from the Roy Rogers Show. We rode around like any other kids in the neighborhood me singing and Clancy wishing I would just shut up. At first we only rode on dirt driveways, farm roads and in the fields. Then came the true test of my ability, skill, and courage. Clancy decided that I was ready, I could ride on the highway. Never once did I doubt that my brother was always looking out for my best interest. During the time we rode together on the trails and dirt roads around the fields. I would frequently fall, and he would pick me up and tell me to quit crying and send me on my way again. So on my first road trip I never questioned his instructions. I knew that my older brother was taking care of me and teaching me to ride. Clancy gave me instructions that day that I remember as though it were yesterday. "Ok Buddy he said, ride down the highway to the cross roads and back" a distance of probably a half mile or so. And "oh yeah Buddy those lines down the center of the road are for bicycles. Always try and keep your bike tires on that white line when you ride on the highway". Off down the highway I went singing my heart out "happy trails to you until we meet again", with my wheels on that little white line, horns were honking and people waving at me, cars swerving to the side of the road, but I was happy I could ride; just like my big brother had taught me.

Clancy also taught me to swim a little later in our lives but, that's an entirely different story.

FIRST GRADE KERMAN

By the time I was 6 and ready for 1st grade I was way ahead of most kids my age in my ability to play ball, fight, jump and run because of my association with my brother and his friends all being four years or more older than me. These older kids taught me so much more than I should have known at my age. The down side however, is that I was taught nothing about school. A kid my age should have known more about school subjects such as numbers and letters than I did.

I'm not sure why Dad did this or why he had the following conversation with me. But before I started school he instilled in me a few very basic behavioral traits that I was instructed to take to school with me. It's possible I may have taken some of these a little too literal. Which may explain some of my problems. It's also possible that six may have been too young to really understand what he was trying to teach me. In any event, these are the guidelines he taught me. As well as the consequences that were attached to each one prior to starting class in the first grade.

1) If anyone ever calls you a dirty name you hit them and hit them hard. You hit them square in the face just as hard and as fast as you can. When people call you these names they are calling your mother a name as well, and we won't allow that. I'm not sure if he meant Evelyn or Grandma), and it

really wouldn't have mattered I hit them anyway and I had permission to do it.

2) Never start a fight; but if you have to fight you better win because you will get a spanking when you get home and it will be worse if you lose.

3) Never run from a fight. If I find out you are a coward I will take all the hide off your back side. I will not have a coward in this family. Something he repeated to me again in the 9th grade.

4) If you get in trouble at school and get a spanking you will get a worse spanking when you get home.

From my perspective, and looking back it is evident that this was a no win situation.

Now that I'm older I think what Dad was trying to teach me is that if you're going to fight, as kids do, it had better be worth the trouble you will get into at home. I, on the other hand, quickly learned that all I needed to say was that so-in so called me a dirty name any dirty name to me had implications of my mother's reputation and I was pretty much in the clear. The trouble at home was not all that bad. I had found an acceptable reason to fight and I was only six years old.

When I started school there was a kid who from the very first day in school he would call me that name or some other name that I translated to mean the same and I would clobber him. I never lost a fight to him but I saw the principle quite often. This kid must have been really dumb. Because he just kept doing the same thing repeatedly almost every day he would call me a name and I would beat him up. Then get into trouble with the teacher and the principle. Perhaps I wasn't so smart either. The problem that I faced was that he lived in town in a real house and had parents with some kind of attachment to the community. While I was a migrants' child, who didn't have real parents. I lived with my grandparents and we had no community attachments. Therefore, I would get in trouble almost every day. It soon became common knowledge that I was the toughest guy in first grade so some of the second graders wanted to have a go at me as well. I admit I did very well but there was one kid in the 2nd grade who I frequently fought with, however, we never got to finish the fight. We would always wrestle and kick and punch then someone would break us up and off to the principle we would go. I think the teachers and staff had pretty much singled me out as a trouble maker by then. But, to my credit; I was not a bully. I never was a bully and I don't believe I actually started any fights. But I wasn't about to run either. I never liked the type of person that picked on smaller children even then. I'm pretty sure Dad was getting tired of wearing out the seat of my pants and he didn't think things were going to get any better unless I had the chance to finish this fight once and for all. One day I was informed that Dad was going to take me to this kid's house and I was going to fight him until one of us gave in and admitted defeat. After that he never wanted to hear any more about me fighting in school for any reason. Dad sat me down before we left and explained the rules of the fight to me. Simple; I had to win. If I lost he was going to give me a spanking like no other spanking I had ever had. I think he said "I'm going to hit you so hard your shirt tail is going to roll up like a window blind" (He said that often). So off we went. Dad, Clancy and I to this kid's house (another family with community attachments). I have no idea what Dad told his father but they agreed and put us in the fenced in yard and turned us loose. I think my fear of the whipping I would get for losing was motivation enough not to lose and I didn't. However, shortly after that we were told that I was being removed from Kerman School and could not return. I think the phrase used was "Buddy just don't fit in at this school you should try someplace else". There I was, probably the only kid anyone knew that was kicked out of first grade for fighting.

We moved to a small place just outside of town and I rode the bus each day to a small school in the country. Personally I thought I was doing pretty well at this school. At least as far as I can recall.

Although I still had a bit of a temper and could not tolerate anyone teasing or making fun of me for any reason. On one particular occasion when I had the measles and red spots all over my face and body. My brother Clancy started teasing me about it. I knew I couldn't whip him in a fair fight so I picked up a butcher knife from the kitchen and chased him into the yard. As he was running away I threw the knife as hard as I could but it only hit him in the foot. Of course he screamed and Mom gave me a pretty harsh beating for throwing the knife at my brother. I was still very angry and as soon as she quit spanking me and left the house again. I decided to show every one of them just how unfair it was that I got a spanking and he was not punished for teasing me. I got a box of matches from the stove and set the curtains that were used to cover the cupboards where we kept canned goods and dishes on fire. There was a lot of smoke but no real damage. This time Mom told me to "just wait till your Dad gets home". This meant that she was going to let Dad administer the discipline. He whipped me again when he got home. In my opinion this was also unfair.

However, I knew better than to do anything stupid this time. I may not have been so angry and I would have taken my punishment more willingly, if I had actually stuck the knife in his back as I had intended. However, it was lucky for him that due to my size I couldn't throw it that far or that hard so I merely got him in the foot.

At some point during that year while living in the same house, Dad brought home a puppy for me. He may have been trying to make me feel better about being bitten earlier by Clancy's dog after Clancy told him to attack me. I don't think Clancy thought he would actually attack me, but I was bitten none the less. The dog Dad brought home for me was so small that Dad carried him home in his shirt pocket. I named him PEE WEE. He was my constant companion for six years until he was accidentally ran over by a friends bicycle when we were going over jumps to see how high we could get.

I finished 1st grade at this school and started the 2nd grade. Then something unfortunate happened. It happened while my class was playing a game called "Duck, Duck Grey Duck" we were playing at recess with our teacher's supervision. In this game boys and girls were in a circle and someone on the outside of the circle would walk around the circle tapping each person on the head and saying Duck-Duck -Duck and eventually he or she would say Gray Duck as they tapped that person. Then they would run around the circle being chased by the one they had just tapped. That person would chase them back to the void spot created in the circle. If you caught them before they got back to the open spot they were out and the circle got progressively smaller. For whatever the reason when this boy tapped me on the head he also deliberately stomped on my hand. The chase ensued and when he returned to the void I had created by chasing him I promptly smacked him in the mouth for stomping on my hand. The teacher came across the circle and slapped me hard across the face. Without a thought (pure reflex) I hit her as hard as I could. Of course I could only reach her belly. It truly was a reflex on my part. I would have hit anyone that hit me the way she did without a moment's hesitation. I immediately realized that I was in some kind of serious trouble. My brother had hit his teacher for slapping him only a few weeks previously but that teacher was a man. This was entirely different, we weren't supposed to hit girls. I did the only thing I could think of at the time; I ran. I ran as far and as fast as my little legs would take me. I left the school and ran through the country over, irrigation canals and across roads and through open fields. I wasn't sure even how to get home, but I ran anyway. I wanted to put as much distance between me and that teacher as I could. I knew; without a doubt that I was in trouble. Trouble like I had never been in before. I not only had just hit a teacher, I had hit a female teacher. I had no idea if Mom and Dad were still out working in a field and even if they were I wouldn't have had a clue as to which field they might be in. I wanted to get to them and explain what had happened before anyone else. I knew I would get a spanking, not only for hitting my classmate, but for sure I would get it big time for hitting my teacher. Somehow I managed to find our house. I ran into the yard scared, tired and crying in fear of what I knew was about to happen to me. Mom and Dad weren't home. That made things even worse. Now I had time to think. In my mind I could imagine all that was going to happen when they did return. I was still crying, and scared of what I feared was going to happen when they came in from the fields at the end the day. But surprisingly enough, I didn't get the whipping I expected. When the teacher hit me. She had hit me so hard the mark on the side of my face and head was still red and swollen when Mom and Dad came home. Her hand print was still visible on the side of my face. I didn't realize until then that Mom took a very dim view of any other adult, teachers included, hitting us in the head. I found out that evening just exactly how strongly she felt about it. There was some kind of school meeting that night which parents were invited to attend and meet the teachers. This is where teachers talk about how well all the kids were doing and that sort of thing. Mom decided to attend and to take me with her to the meeting. I assumed I was to apologize and let the teacher tell her side of the story and then I would get the whipping I had coming when we got back home. When we arrived at school she first showed the marks still evident on my face to the principle. Then she took me to the teacher and showed her my face, and said something to the effect of "so you like to slap little boys in the side of the head hard enough to make their ears hurt and leave horrible marks". "Let me show you what it feels like". At which point she hit that teacher in the face so hard she sent her sprawling across the room in front of everyone. We left the meeting that night with Mom's final words to my teacher. "Now you know how he felt".

While I may not have been kicked out of second grade I think we saw it coming again. So we left before someone else said "Buddy just doesn't fit in at this school".

HOLLISTER CA.

I'm not sure why Mom got so angry about someone else hitting me in the head; Mom did it several times herself and thought nothing of it. However it wasn't the normal way of discipline. Normal whippings were administered on the back side but were not limited to just our butts. One particular time when we were living in Hollister, California where we had gone to pick cherries. There was a woman and Mom who were talking as I stood by her side and the lady asked "when is your old man coming home". Mom responded with some answer and I responded with "yeah the old man will be home at "I never finished the sentence she backhanded me and lifted me clean off the ground. I was told "never refer to your Dad as the old man again" and I never did, at least not when I could be heard.

We were paid by the pound to pick cherries in Hollister, the more you picked the more money you made. Each of us was expected to pick and contribute to the family income. Cherries were pulled from the tree and placed in a bucket. Sometimes with the stem attached and sometimes without. Without stems was referred to as milking cherries. The buckets we put them in hung from a harness around your neck and once filled they were weighed by the owner or field boss and you were paid accordingly. Clancy and I both had a quota of cherries that we were expected to pick each day. After that we were free to do whatever we wished. We enjoyed going to a small stream close by and would play in the water. We would chase the

ducks that were not quite old enough to fly and when we were lucky
we actually killed a few with rocks. We would bring them back to
camp and would have duck for dinner. We also caught frogs with
our hands or with a three pronged spear on a long pole called a "frog
gig". Clancy and I would hunt frogs at night with a flashlight and
the gig. I was not yet strong enough to handle the gig on the long
pole but I would hold the flashlight while he speared the frogs. You
had to hold the light very steady because if the light left the frogs
eyes they would jump in the water and disappear. We made a great
team and actually enjoyed the hunting of frogs together. We ate the
frog legs which was a major supplement to our family diet. During
the day Clancy always picked his quota of cherries and was done by
noon. I on the other hand really liked to eat cherries. I would pick
some then eat a bunch and repeat the process over and over. Often
I wouldn't even have one bucket full of cherries by the time Clancy
had reached his quota. For whatever the reason on this particular
day the old man (I can call him that now) decided it was time I got
a little more serious about working. He set a ladder in a tree and
informed me that if I did not pick a bucket full of cherries he was
going to take one of those cherry limbs and take all of the hide off
my back side. I knew how much that would hurt. I'd had many
spankings of this nature before for various things, so I climbed up
that ladder and I picked cherries like a mad man. I would pick a
bunch and push them down to make room for more. I was going
to make Dad proud. I repeated this process over and over until the
bucket of cherries was so heavy I could hardly drag it over to the
boss to be weighed. I can't remember what a bucket of cherries was
supposed to weigh. Maybe ten pounds or so. Whatever it was, my
bucket of cherries was at least twice as heavy. The boss called Dad
over thinking I had put a rock or something in the bucket. When
they emptied the contents of my bucket, squished cherries and cherry
juice ran everywhere. I was very proud of my bucket, but Dad was
absolutely furious. It probably goes without saying he thought I had
done that on purpose to embarrass him in front of the boss. I still

got the hide on my backside worn thin. Sometimes you just can't seem to win. Later during my early teenage years Dad and I talked of this and he still thought I had done it on purpose. I suppose I should probably point out that to the best of my knowledge I probably averaged a spanking every other day until I was about 12 years old. When I got my last whipping from Dad (I'll tell about that later). I can also say, without a doubt I deserved some type of punishment for most of my actions and my smart mouth. At that time spankings were not frowned upon as they are today. In fact I believe they were probably encouraged as an acceptable means of discipline by your teachers as well as your parents. I even got an occasional spanking from my friend's parents as well. Even that was ok at the time. I think everyone took the "spare the rod and spoil the child" reference quite literally. It wasn't that I was really all that bad. It's just that I had a bit of an attitude. I will mention some of the more memorable spankings or paddling's that were dealt to me as we progress through this story only because at times there was a bit of humor as to why I got the spanking. Looking back it must have been funny to watch me get a whipping since Dad being right handed would always grab my left arm and as he would spank me with whatever implement he chose. He and I would go around in circles as he hit me. And I would try to arch my back and attempt to scoot my rear end out of the reach of his hand, belt or switch. Of course I couldn't, but we would go round and round in circles with me yelling "I'm sorry Daddy I won't do it again". I always said the same thing. And Dad saying "are you going to straighten up or do I have to take all the hide off your back. "

Once when I was older he told me to go get a switch so I could receive my allotted punishment. Being the smart aleck that I was I came back with a twig that was maybe a 1/8" of an inch in diameter. Dad lost his temper and told me to go get a switch and do it quickly, and that I had better get it right this time. Still the kid with the smart attitude, I came back with an apple limb. It was about two inches in diameter. I didn't think he would hit me with this either but he lost it. He took that from me and that's exactly what I got my spanking with. I never repeated that stunt again. A lesson learned; be careful what you ask for, you might get it.

DINGVILLE, CALIFORNIA USA

After Hollister I think we moved to a place that no one believes exists. However, to prove its existence I took my wife to Dingville when she and I were living in California on one of my assignments while working for the Department of Defense (DoD). When my wife and I went there it looked pretty much as I remembered one building and a sign saying "Welcome to Dingville". Like so many other places I lived as a child that one building was a bar.

Dingville is not really a town but more like an area about 25 miles from Marysville, and Yuba City, California. Two towns that are situated on the junction of the Feather and Yuba Rivers. Dingville, California was where I attended part of the 2nd and 3rd grades.

We lived in a one room shack once more. It had electricity and nothing else. There was a well with a hand pump outside. We were working in a peach orchard owned by a Christian family. I remember they had two daughters and that they were Nazarene by faith. I remember that only because one daughter was named Emerald and I thought that was a pretty name. She made fun of me because I had picked and eaten nectarines in my life and I continually got the two confused. Nazarene or nectarine how would I know I was only about seven. So I insisted on calling their family Nectarines. For the most part; life on the peach ranch was good. Clancy and I worked when we weren't in school and if we had all of our allotted work completed we went fishing on the Feather River. We caught perch, bass and bluegills. We found a dilapidated old boat on a slew by the river and with one of us continuously bailing out of the water that would leak into the boat we were able to keep it afloat. At night we could go the river or walk along the irrigation ditch beside our cabin and gig frogs just as we had done in Hollister. Mom and Dad purchased potatoes and beans and hamburger as well as lunch meat and eggs, but the majority of our food especially meat, we either caught, stabbed, or shot. There was no refrigerator only an ice box. The ice man came by about once or twice a week and dropped off a huge block of ice. I remember thinking he must have been the strongest man in the world to carry those big blocks of ice from his truck across the road and over a small foot bridge to our cabin. Often he would knock off a small piece of ice and give it to us to suck on as it melted in our hands or mouth. Remember in the Christmas story from Kerman I told you that Clancy also taught me to swim? It was while living in this house that he taught me to swim. Since we didn't have running water we obviously did not have a shower or a bath tub either. Clancy and I discovered that if we took a bar of soap to the irrigation canal we could go swimming under the guise of taking a bath. We did this as often as possible and our favorite place was by the bridge. The bridge was probably 8 to 10 ft above the water and the kids from around the area would jump off the bridge and swim to the bank using weeds or bushes to pull themselves up the steep bank and out of the water. The water was swift and deep and I would only go in as long as I could hold on to a bush and I could splash around with one hand while the other clung tightly to whatever plant would support me. I'm not sure what made Clancy decide that this was the day I needed to learn to swim; but it was time. He grabbed hold of me and said "I'm tired of my little brother being called a chicken". Then he not so gently picked me up and threw me off the bridge into the cold, deep and swift moving water. I was terrified. Maybe he was aware of something I wasn't. I think he may have believed that all kids will dog paddle to the bank. It's just something we are born with. When he threw me in he said "now swim you little chicken or you're going to drown". I swam! I dog paddled to the bank and I managed to pull myself out of the water. This process was repeated several times until he was satisfied that I was convinced that I wasn't going to drown. Probably not the best way to learn to swim but it was effective. Later in our life he shared with me that Dad had taught him to swim the same way.

I wish my family would have purchased stock in the Lifebuoy Soap factory during this time in my life, we could be rich today. I had a vocabulary that was not exactly acceptable for a 7 or 8 year old. Mom's remedy for swearing was to wash those dirty words out of your mouth. I ate so much soap I used to think I was keeping that company in business. I was good at repeating what I had heard in the fields. And since I had a brother who was older I would also repeat the words he and his friends used as well. From that perspective you could say that Clancy was also very instrumental in my advanced use of the English Language.

Dad worked for this family as the only full time worker and was more or less running the place. As I said he was a hard worker and his efforts were appreciated by the owner. So much so that when their family had to move to Palm Springs and a warmer, dryer climate for the health of a family member (I think it was the farmer's wife.) They ask Dad to stay and care for the place in their absence. He would be the only employee running the farm and acting just as though the owner was still there. They also ask if we would move into their house furniture and all. So for the very first time in my life; I lived in a regular house. It had a yard with grass and a really big oak tree with shade and a swing in the front yard. It also had a fig tree in the back. The house wasn't some fantastic dream house, but it was a mansion compared to anything I had previously lived in. An added bonus is that Clancy and I had a bedroom that we shared. It was the first time that we had our own room. Prior to this we had always lived in one room cabins and had never had a bedroom that wasn't just a sheet or blanket separating us from Mom and Dad. Clancy and I were always expected to work and our income went to support the family. We were allowed to keep a small portion of our earnings and we never questioned it. I had been working to some degree since I had dragged that first cotton sack through the fields back when I was five. Giving your income to the head of the house was a tradition among many migrant families. If you didn't like the circumstance you were always free to leave. I never met a family that didn't do the same thing or something similar to that during my time of growing up in the fields. It was just the way it was, and rarely was it questioned. Sharing my income with the family was what I did for as long as my dad was alive and I was living under his roof.

DINGVILLE SCHOOL

Clancy and I went to a small country school not far from Dingville that had two buildings. One building for first through fourth grades and one for grades five through eight.

There may have been a kindergarten but I don't remember. I did well in this school Mom got a job cooking in the kitchen and my teacher soon realized that while most 2nd graders knew the alphabet. I was the exception. I hadn't a clue what A, B, C meant or even why anyone would want to memorize them. I was informed that I would be required to memorize the alphabet in order to advance to the next level in school. I learned them by putting together a puzzle. I was good at puzzles and I had them memorized in no time at all. I was soon in the process of catching up to with other children of that age. I was only in one fight at that school that I can recall, and because of that fight I learned what "swats" were. This was made painfully aware to me by a principle (also the 5th-8th grade teacher) whom I believe had considerable experience in this area. He brought the other kid and me to the front of the class of 5th-8th graders. He told me to bend over and gave me a swat to my back side with a wooden paddle that made a loud crack and hurt so stinking much I wanted to cry. Did I mention before that I had a bit of an attitude? There was no way I was going to cry in front of all those big kids. I decided the best response was for me to just say "thank you" and then I sat down in the waste basket as though I were cooling off my butt. When my partner in crime got his swat he repeated what I had just done. The same thing "thank you" and then took my place in the waste basket. I'm not sure if the principle got angry or was amused. However, I soon regretted my actions. He looked right at me and said "so if you liked that so much bend over". "I'll give you another one ". I really doubt he hit me much harder than he did on the first swat but I know it hurt like crazy and there was no stopping the tears this time. Both of us had big tears running down our cheeks and dripping from our chin. We forgot the embarrassment of being in front of the older kids and just stood there until we were dismissed. Not a single word of thanks was uttered from either one of us. The sympathy I received from the older girls at recess was the only thing that made any of it seem worthwhile. Of course I got another whipping from Dad for fighting when I got home.

Mom and Dad continued to drink as always. However, for the most part there were fewer fights and we weren't left in the car as much as before. But then by their standards Clancy was old enough to watch me if we stayed at home. It was a mix, sometimes we went to the bar with them, and sometimes we stayed at home. At this point we were also tasked with doing the dishes and we received $.25 cents for doing them. Clancy being older decided that he should skip his turn at doing dishes and he would let me take his turn. For that privilege it seemed only fair that he would give me a nickel and he of course would keep $0.20 for being so generous. This seemed fair to me and this arrangement continue until the folks discovered it and made him stop taking advantage of my immaturity. I relayed this story to my children and when they met my brother for the first time one of them asked him" why did you take all of my Dad's money". He had no idea what they were referring to but a quick explanation gave us all a good laugh.

One of the favorite places Mom and Dad liked to go to on the weekends was a country bar that had the word OAKS in the name. It was Twin Oaks or Three Oaks or maybe Five Oaks. It was here that I mentioned earlier where Mom decked some guy with a bottle that was used in those days to put bulk oil in your car. Not sure what the guy said or did but he turned his back long enough for her to pick up that heavy bottle by the metal spout attached to it and whack him over the bean. Then she looked at me and said go get your Dad. At the time Dad was in a garage owned by some backyard mechanic. He came running out, but nothing ensued and the guy left a little bloody and a little dazed.

It was in this same bar a few weeks later that I will describe in some detail a very violent fight between Dad and another man. I will describe this particular fight because it becomes a very important milestone later in the lives of our family.

In just a few short weeks. Our lives as we had always known, were about to change. I don't know what started the fight. It had something to do with Mom and some guy bothering her but again she told me to go get your Dad. I did and by the time my Dad walked into the bar he was already angry. He and this other man went outside, Dad was not aware that the guy had pulled a knife while he was going out the door. He cut Dad above the eye with the knife and it bled pretty badly. As I said earlier head wounds bleed profusely and Dad had blood running freely down his face, into his eyes and all over his clothes. I think Dad was madder than I had ever seen him and certainly more violent. I'm not sure if he was furious because the man pulled a knife or because of whatever Mom had told him that had actually started the fight in the first place. Fortunately the guy with the knife was not all that good at using it. If he were he could have done more serious damage and the fight would have ended abruptly. But he missed his chance and Dad was furious. Once outside Dad avoided the knife and when he hit the man in the side of the head he went down and stayed down. When this man hit the ground my Dad commenced to kick him like he was going for a field goal. Dad kept kicking him over and over while the man tried to cover his face and body but eventually he was unconscious and could no longer defend himself at all. Dad still kept kicking him even then. It took several men from the bar to pull Dad off and restrained him. We went to a hospital in either Marysville or Yuba City where Dad had stiches to close up the eye but other than that one cut from the knife Dad was ok. The other man however had to be taken by ambulance to the hospital. We never heard anything more about him other than he had gone to the hospital, and he was not in good shape. We were back at work again on Monday morning with life continuing as normal. Another day in the field and orchards.

TRANSFORMATION

As Paul Harvey, radio commentator used to say "and now for the rest of the story".

Where do I go from here? I can't tell you what to think or how to feel about what you are about to read. However, just try and keep an open mind.

The following event took place about a month or so after the fight that I have just described. To me it is an amazing event that has stuck with me through the years and impacted my life and who I am. For now forget about the abuse, the fights and the abandonment by parents. Even the separation of siblings is inconsequential at this point. For now focus on what I am about to describe and the circumstances surrounding the day. The day started like any other day. Dad went to work in the peach orchard, working completely alone as he did every day. He was the farmer's only employee. It had to be spring of 1954 because he was thinning peaches and that is done in the spring while the fruit is still green on the tree. A process where the fruit was removed from the tree when it was small and green. The peaches are spaced far enough apart so that the weight of the fruit as they ripen and grow will not break the limbs. This process also made for a larger healthier peach when they matured. Mom wasn't with him in the field this day. She had gotten to the point where she rarely worked the fields and going up and down a ladder was extremely difficult and painful for her. She may have still been working in the school kitchen at that time. So to set the scene correctly let me stress once more, that Dad was completely alone in that orchard not a single solitary person was out there but him. He had been out there all day by himself in the tree just thinning peaches minding his own business. He came in from the field that evening at the normal quitting time. Mom had dinner on the table as she usually would if she wasn't working. We all sat down and Dad looked at each one of us bowed his head raised his hands and said "Hallelujah! Today I found Jesus". Clancy and I looked at each other wondering who that was. Dad tried to explain it to us. However, we were confused and really had no idea what he was talking about. We weren't actually sure we wanted to know anyway. However, from that very moment forward I never saw my dad touch another drink, another cigar or cigarette or tobacco of any form. Never again did he argue with Mom. He would simply walk away and pray. For whatever the reason with no explanation something amazing happened in that peach tree. Something that I would not understand until years later. It truly was a transformation of some sort. Think about it as I go forward with my story, he was completely alone in a tree; not another person in sight. I mean he had no one to talk to. No wayward stranger wandering through the orchard stopping to ask if he could take a minute to let him tell Dad about Jesus. He was all alone. All by himself. He didn't see another person all day. This can't be said or described any other way. And yet to me this event has had great significance in my life over the years. In the New Testament of the Bible in Acts Chapter 9 there is the story of Saul. A man whose life had been dedicated to persecuting the followers of Jesus. God struck him with a blinding light as he was walking to Damascus. God spoke to him and he became a follower of Christ preaching and spreading the gospel. Dad didn't become temporarily blind. And I'm not going to say he heard God physically speak. However, something happened in that tree and it was for the better. Never have I seen a man more dedicated to prayer and his belief in God than my dad was from that very moment. Instead of bars on Friday or Saturday night we went to church, all of us, every Sunday.

I would like to say that everything became instantly better and that we lived a story book life from that point on. But that would be a lie. The scars in my life before this were deep enough and the memories so vivid that as a teen or even preteen I rebelled both against the authority of God and of men. I know I was a problem for my dad. I tried his patience every day of his life. And yet he continued to pray for my life.

We still struggled financially but we were doing ok as a family. Life was good. I even had a birthday party with some of my school mates. I had received a BB gun and I would spend my days hunting anything that had wings or could run. I mostly hunted grasshoppers they were large and abundant and I would practice shooting them to prepare for those times that a bird would let me get close enough to make them a good target. I killed a lot more hoppers than birds. Over all, things were pretty normal. Mom still would become argumentative on occasion but it happened less and less with no alcohol in the picture. I think Dad did very well adapting to our new life. But then, he was the one in the tree, Mom, struggled some, but to her credit she tried hard to become what was expected of a Pentecostal Woman. Dad had decided that the Pentecostal Church of God is where we would attend. And so we did; usually three services a week. One during the week and two on Sunday. I attended Sunday school, memorized verses and was able to win my first Bible with my name engraved on the front. I was one proud kid and Dad was proud of me also. The Pentecostal Church believes in speaking in tongues and an Amen or Hallelujah during the sermon is not at all considered disruptive.

As stated earlier things were a lot easier but we were still poor by most standards of American finance. Our diet was the same as it always had been. We ate a lot of potatoes, rice (because it was grown close by and was cheap or free), beans, eggs, bread and lunch meat of various types. If we had meat it was hamburger or whatever wild game we happen to catch or kill (usually rabbits, frogs and a lot of fish.) This was our diet and it remained pretty much the same throughout my growing years. However, Sunday afternoon potlucks at the church was by far a favorite time for Clancy and me. We could usually have all the fried chicken, various casseroles or pie that we could eat. This was true of all the Pentecostal churches that we attended during our youth.

There is no way I can take Dad's conversion lightly. He lived the life he proclaimed every single day until his death. He was in fact a follower of Jesus just as Saul who became the Apostle Paul was also a follower of Christ. As I stated in the beginning this was not to be about faith or religion. At least it was not intended to be. But it is important to understand that this was a life changing event for everyone in this family. I would also love to tell you that I fell quickly into Dad's footsteps. That my struggle to determine who or what I was going to be was over, or that I was no longer a problem child but that would not be true.

We continued to live on the ranch for a time and not a lot happened. In fact looking back it was a very happy time for me. Oh sure I still got into trouble and Dad would wear my backside out about every other day or so for something I did or didn't do. I learned to drive the tractor and the jeep in the orchards by the time I was eight. I also learned that no matter how hard I tried I couldn't fly. If you remember earlier I said we never believed in Santa Claus. However, I did believe in Superman. I was allowed to put a towel around my neck and run through the orchards yelling "up, up and away". Just like superman did on the radio and in the movies. One day I had the idea that if I started out from a higher elevation I would have a better chance at flying. I climbed to the top of a ladder that was in the orchard with towel pinned tightly around my neck and with a hearty "Up, Up and Away" I dove off. I stretched my body out as far as I could go; arms out hoping to fly. I came down flat out on my stomach in the mud of an irrigated orchard. I wasn't hurt at least not physically. However it was my last attempt to fly. Just think if Mom would have told me that Santa was real and superman a fake, it all could have been avoided. Santa or no Santa we did get a Christmas tree that year and continued with a tree for many years after that as well.

CHICAGO

In the summer of 1955 for some reason known only to Dad it was decided that when the peach harvest was over we were all going to Chicago and see my uncle Richard, Evelyn's brother. He had left California at some point and moved to Chicago. He divorced his first wife the one who we were told wouldn't let him keep Buzzy. And he married a second wife named Jo. We were going to take our beat up old car and drive from California to Chicago. A place I had never heard of but it sounded far away.

I'm not totally sure why we went to Chicago other than to see their son. However, I suspect the motivation for this trip had a lot to do with Dad wanting the opportunity to tell Richard about Jesus and about the dramatic change in our lives.

We drove for days camping out along the road as we went. Stopping to see any sight that seemed worthy of a road trip in 1955. I know we stopped at Salt Lake City, where we saw the Mormon Tabernacle. Clancy and I both swam in the Great Salt Lake floating around feeling the buoyancy and the sensation of not being able to sink. We stopped at Little America and was rewarded with free ice water and an ice cream cone. We went through the Rocky Mountains camping and fishing along the way. We must have gone through Wisconsin at some point because we caught fireflies, something we had never seen before. Clancy and I spent hours every evening chasing them and putting them in a quart jar to make a flashlight, then releasing them before morning. This trip was a kids dream. We never once spent the night in a hotel or ate at a restaurant. We had a lot of experience camping during our lives and it came in handy during this trip.

When Mom and Dad went to visit a relative it was never a quick trip. We had spent a long time getting to Chicago, and we were planning to stay a significant amount of time as well. It was what we always did when visiting the few relatives we had. Or at least the few we claimed or that claimed us. Clancy and I met with the family of Richard and his wife Jo. There were cousins our age and we readily became part of the group of guys and gals roaming the street, running through the alley's and killing rats with baseball bats as they fed on the garbage left in the garbage cans throughout Chicago. Of course kids get in fights and we were no exception. There were several fights but, it didn't take long to understand that fighting in Chicago was not the same as a small country school in rural California. One particular fight that I remember well was because I got my rear end kicked, and lost Twenty dollars at the same time. I was playing with some boy I had just met. I noticed a twenty dollar bill laying in the alley and I picked it up and showed this kid what I had found. I told him I was going to share with him. Ten bucks each. I guess that wasn't what he had in mind. He beat me up pretty bad and then took the whole twenty dollars. I never ran across the kid again. If I had I doubt I would have tried to regain my twenty. However, I'm certain Clancy would have taken from him whatever money he may have had on him at the time.

We also went to Lake Michigan to fish and to Buckingham Fountain, Brookfield Zoo and to my favorite place, The Museum of Science and Industry. All went really well for some time while we were there. I think Dad and Uncle Richard had plans for Dad and Mom to stay in Chicago. Dad could get a job unloading trucks and he could continue to tell Richard and his family about the peace he had found through Christ in the peach orchard. However, it didn't happen that way and it was all my fault.

I was playing with a bat and ball in the school yard (that's where you went if you weren't in the alley) I would throw the ball in the air hit it then go get it and hit it back the other way continually repeating the process. Some little kid probably about six, said that if I would hit the ball he would run and fetch it. Sounded like a good deal to me. We did this several times and I noticed he was trying to anticipate my swing and starting forward before I could swing. Each time I would have to stop my swing to prevent hitting him. This was getting to be annoying. I warned him that if he continued doing that, I was going to hit him in the head with the bat. He must have thought I was joking. Because sure enough I tossed the ball in the air he stepped forward and I hit him in the head. I may not have been real big but I could swing a bat. The sound a bat makes when it strikes a skull is sickening. The instantaneous blood flow makes it all but impossible to see exactly how much damage was done. I knew however that I had hurt this kid pretty badly. There was blood squirting out the side of his head. I picked him up in my arms not knowing what to do when some older kids told me his parents were in a bar about a block or so down the street. I carried him in my arms that entire distance. By the time I had reached the bar we were both covered in blood. It must have been a shocking sight for the parents. They immediately took him from me and went to the closest hospital. I on the other hand went back to the house and told everyone what I had done. It may not have seemed so bad to the adults involved had I not admitted that I had warned the kid I was going to hit him in the head, and then I actually did it. Mom, Dad and I went to the hospital and found the parents, who had summoned the police. Because I had willingly carried this kid to his parents rather than leaving him lay in the school yard, I was not being charged or accused of anything malicious. However, the police told Dad that the best thing we could do at this point was to leave town as soon as we could before the parents decided to try and get money from us, for doctor and hospital bills that would be incurred to repair the damage.

I don't think anyone really wanted to leave, but since the police suggested we leave, I guess it was time to go. We left that evening as soon as we could pack the car and say our goodbyes. All the fun we had on our trip going to Chicago I still remember well. Yet I don't remember a single thing about the trip back to California and the peach orchard. We never heard from the kid or the parents again. Uncle Richard said in a letter they had contacted him once but he didn't admit to having any knowledge of where we had gone.

When we returned to the farm the owner was living in the main house so we again occupied the little one room cabin. We also returned to the Pentecostal Church in Marysville, California where we were attending before we left. Everything seemed to be back to normal and when school started I was in the 3rd grade.

THE MOVE TO WASHINGTON

I'm not sure what made Dad decide to move from California to Washington but I think he felt that God was calling him to return to the Yakima Valley. He had lived there as a child and he and mom had also lived there for a while during the depression. I do know that whatever the reason he wanted to leave California it turned out to be a good decision. We left in late fall of 1955 shortly after Thanksgiving. Less than a month later the part of California we had just left received greater than usual amounts of rain and in December of 1955 the dike on the Feather River gave way and there was severe flooding in the Sacramento Valley. The entire area was under water. Trees, orchards and houses were all displaced by the flood. We were told the house we had once occupied was washed downstream approximately five miles. Dad said "I felt that God wanted us to leave."

After Christmas break I enrolled in Naches Grade School. I would continue to bounce back and forth between Naches Grade School and Lower Naches Grade School for the remainder of my grade school years until I enrolled at Naches High School as a freshman in 1960.

That first year in Naches as a third grader was pretty uneventful for all of us. Dad had found a church and I was doing well in school with a few minor exceptions. I still occasionally got in a fight but by now I had learned to pick the toughest kid in class during your first week in a new school and go for it. Even if you lost you had earned a certain degree of respect from everyone except your new teacher. However, for the most part no one else would mess with you the rest of the year. Actually my brother Clancy probably told me to do that hoping I'd get my rear end kicked. I did however find myself spending a significant time in the classroom closet. I certainly felt I was put there more often than I should have been. I was put there for any number of reasons (mostly for not listening). One time stands out above all others. It was my first semester in Naches as a 3rd grader and I was told to go into the closet during story time. Usually female teachers used story time or recess for punishment. Our classroom closet was a large room that was used to keep books, paper, and art supplies. As well as just about anything else you could imagine they would store in the closet. On this particular day I found a bottle of rubber cement. We had used rubber cement previously in art class and I was aware that you could put some in the palm of your hand and as it dried it had the ability to be rolled into little rubber balls. If you added more it would dry and the ball just kept getting bigger. There was a time in our society in the 1970s or 1980s when the in thing for kids to do was sniff glue. During that era I of all people understood the significance and the outcome of inhaling the toxic fumes of glue. When my teacher came to get me after story time. She opened the closet door and I literally fell out of the closet. I was stoned. I also got sick, I stumbled out of there glassy eyes and pale complexion. I'm sure I must have really looked awful. I can look back at this now and laugh. However, I bet my teacher was terrified. Just think if she had been reading a novel, I would have been in there an even longer time and I would have really been in bad shape when I emerged. But on the brighter side can you imagine how big that rubber cement ball I was making would have been.

There is one other event at about this time in my life that my wife thinks is hilarious. Clancy and I each received a sample tube of Crest

Toothpaste in the mail. Neither of us had any idea what to do with it because we had never owned a tooth brush. However, being two very resourceful young boys we read the directions about putting it on your teeth. That sounded easy. We put some in our mouths and thought it tasted pretty good so we ate the entire two tubes. Fortunately they were small tubes and there were no side effects to eating a sample tube of Crest. Just for the record, Crest is still my choice of tooth paste.

We moved back and forth between Lower Naches and Naches several times during the next few years. Always living in some little house having very few or no indoor amenities. Therefore, this seems as good a place as any to mention the dreaded outhouse. I hated those things. Almost every house we had ever lived in had an outhouse. They always smelled terrible. If you looked down that hole it was a very long way down to that messy part in the bottom. I'm not sure if you could ever have gotten out if you fell through that hole. There were also all kinds of bugs and crawly things. My fear was that if I had to sit down on that little round hole I would either fall in, or a spider would bite me on the butt. If I had to go to the outhouse at night it was always the same scenario. I would force myself to walk to the little square building just to prove I wasn't afraid of the dark. When I was finished I would sprint all the way back to the house catch my breath and walk inside as though all was cool and I had just made a routine visit to the building with the half-moon on the door, and a small board that locked it from the inside and not the outside. My opinion, outhouses still stink and I'm not just referring to the smell.

In one particular house in Lower Naches we had our usual ice box. The one where the ice man delivered ice a couple of times a week. To save money on ice in the winter Dad nailed an apple box on the outside of the window in the kitchen and we had a freezer. We simply opened the window and took out whatever we needed. This house was located on an irrigation canal and access to the place was by a footbridge about two feet wide, no railing for protection and if you tripped or stumbled someone was going to get wet. It's a good thing Clancy had already taught me to swim. While we lived there we ate a lot of rabbits and quail. The rabbits were plentiful and I was allowed to use that same rifle that had been used as a threat to my life numerous times before. However, Clancy would normally do the shooting and I was only allowed to fetch the bunnies and birds. But at times when he wasn't around I was able to prove I wasn't a bad shot and I killed a lot of game to bring to the table.

We moved back to Naches in time to start the 6th grade. We lived in a small house in one of those camps with the cabins on the Naches River. It actually had all of the modern conveniences of the time. It even had a small wire fence surrounding a very small patch of grass. It wasn't fancy but we were doing fine. Dad would work at any farm in the Valley that was hiring at the time. We were members of the local Pentecostal Church of God and by now he was occasionally filling in for a few churches as the Lay Preacher when the normal Preacher was gone or sick. The sixth grade was a time of several major impacts in my life for various reasons. But perhaps the biggest event for me that year was sports. My ability as an athlete was beginning to be noticed. I had been playing ball with my brother and his friends as far back as I can remember. That may very well have been part of the reason that in recess or Physical Education (PE) I excelled more than most my classmates at almost any sport we played. It also had something to do with a God given talent. A talent that as time went by I was able to use to my advantage throughout my life. It was this athletic ability that played a major part in keeping me in school when most people had all but given up on me. Coaches and teachers all agreed that my athletic ability was far beyond my age. So much so that I was asked to play on the school football and baseball teams with the 7th and 8th graders while I was still in the 6th grade. The only baseball glove I had was a first basemen's glove. I may have been the only right fielder to play that position with a first base glove. I didn't care. I got to practice daily and play sometimes, although not often. I also discovered girls and the impact of peer pressure during that year. Both were disastrous. Our teacher a man with a very red bulbous nose and very little patience and handed out swats for almost any offence. Several of my classmates and I decided at some point to see who could get the most swats by the end of the year. We would deliberately antagonize this man and he would hand out swats daily hoping to change our behavior. I don't believe he was ever aware that it was all a contest dreamed up by a bunch of crazy 6th graders. I was in the lead until the last day of school but I finished in second place only because another student volunteered to get an enormous amount of swats on the last day of school. This act of bravery placed him ahead of me in the race for infinite stupidity. No one else was aware that he had taken the lead until it was too late to change the results. He won! No prize or trophy was given to the winner. Only a sore back side and the honor of being the dumbest kids in the 6th grade.

Did I by chance mention at some point previously that I had a bit of an attitude? If not then I'll say it again. I had a quick response for everything. One of the things of that era was to be able to flip someone off, to give them the finger, the dirty digit, the bird, whatever you want to call it, it still meant the same thing. I wanted to be good at presenting that finger at a moment's notice because my brother and all of his friends were very good at it. I would sit at my desk during class and practice by putting a pencil on top of my middle finger and placing my ring finger and index finger on top of the pencil. I mean how cool was that? I got to the point I was able to flip that finger up so fast it was amazing. It was truly impressive; in fact it was almost menacing the way I could do it. I also learned to do it with both hands, simultaneously even. On this particular day (Dad was home so it had to be a weekend), my brother and I got in a fight as we often did and as he was walking out of the yard I popped up that finger so fast. I wanted him to see it. I wanted him to come back and fight me some more even though I knew I would get my butt kicked again. I wanted to make a statement that I wasn't afraid. I was one cool dude and not afraid of anything especially him. This was my way of showing it. At that same time with my finger pointing upward I felt a hot breeze on the back of my neck. Yep, you got it. Dad was standing right behind me and had seen the whole thing. It was not exactly a good position for an eleven year old to be in, and he was certainly not the person I wanted or expected to see me call out my older brother in this particular manner. Remember Dad was a Christian and was very serious about his faith. To him this was a terrible gesture especially coming from his 11 year old son.

The next few seconds went something like this. Dad asked "Buddy what did you just do?"

"Nothing "I replied.

"Don't lie to me I saw you go just like this" and he held up his index finger.

"I did not."

"Don't lie Buddy, I saw you go just like this" and he held up the index finger again.

"I did not! I went just like this." Remember how quick I said I was? He never saw it coming. I flipped that finger up in front of his face so fast that if I had been any closer it would have gone up his nose. I didn't think he would have had time to blink or his mind to register what I had just done. I was wrong. Dad wasn't the only one who didn't see it coming. I never saw it coming either. Before I could even blink. From out of nowhere, and before I could register that I had been hit, Dad hit me in the side of the head so hard I flew off the porch. I rolled across that little piece of grass and up against that wire fence that comprised our yard. In fact were if not for the fence I may have rolled all the way to the driveway.

Then Dad calmly said "go in the house and think about what you just did."

No spanking, nothing at all. I think maybe that was worse. Perhaps Dad felt he'd done enough by knocking me off the porch. I will admit I had it coming. I had just done the unthinkable. I had flipped off my dad. I didn't know what made me do it. I felt awful. I didn't use that finger very often after that as many of my peers did. After that incident it just seemed to be a useless form of communicating my feelings. If I wanted to convey that message to any one I would simply say it, leaving little or no doubt about how I felt about an individual or the situation at hand.

The sixth grade was also the year that I found that my talent as a raft maker was somewhat lacking. The house we lived in was located on the Naches River. It seems strange now, but at that time poor folks lived on the river and endured the possibility of flooding each year. The rich folks and some middle income lived in town and the rest were scattered on farms and ranches around the surrounding hills. Today it seems as though the poor folks live in town, the rich folks are scattered around the hills on acreage with a view and the middle income on the rivers and lower hills, with some of them still living in town.

In any event we lived on the Naches River. Close by our house there was an Island in the river big enough to explore and to camp on. I and a couple of other boys whose names I can't recall, convinced our parents to let us camp there for a night. So we set off with a blanket, a skillet, hatchets, some lard, a sack of potatoes, fishing poles and a box of cookies that someone's mother had thrown in for desert. Our intent was to catch a mess of trout and cook them with the potatoes. We could drink from the river, build a fire, cook our food and have a great time. It would be fun. We set up our camp, started the fire and caught a lot of small trout that made our mouths water just thinking of how tasty they would be. Someone went to the water's edge to clean, peel and wash the potatoes. I have no remembrance of whose idea it was to scrub the potatoes with sand to get them clean. But that is exactly what we did. Cutting them into pieces and cooking them in our skillet of lard until they were almost done. Then came the trout it smelled fantastic. We were ready for a great feast and a great night. However, our gourmet dinner turned south. We very soon realized that when washing the potatoes with sand we had embedded that sand in them. Now it was in the lard and so our fish was also coated with the sand. Every bite we took we could feel and hear the sand grinding in our teeth. We were thankful for the mother that sent the cookies.

The next morning arrived and we were a little hungry but excited about our day on the island. Someone got the idea that if Huck Finn and Tom Sawyer could build a raft and float down the Mississippi River the three of us were capable of building our own raft and floating the Naches River as well. We set out with rope (bailing twine actually) and hatchets and rounded up as many logs as possible for our raft. Tying them together in what we were believed to be sturdy and trustworthy knots. Knots that would have made a boy scout proud. I suppose by about noon our raft was ready and it was time to launch.

The Naches River is a float of probably class 2 rapids in places. Today people raft the river in rubber rafts and kayaks and pay companies for the experience we were about to embark on years before it became a popular activity. We were going to do it with probably a dozen or so logs tied together with twine, a couple of poles to keep us straight with the current and a complete lack of fear or intelligence. Each of us had probably been down parts of the river with inner tubes but that is a little different than a raft perhaps 4-5 feet wide and maybe 6- 8 feet long.

We set out from our island planning on going down river a short distance. Our plan then was to beach the raft and go back to the island. Thinking that maybe at some time we would come back for the raft to continue our adventure another day.

All in all I would say it was a semi successful trip. Less than a quarter mile from the launch point the logs started to come untied. Our knots weren't holding and the logs began to drift away from our raft one at a time with increasing speed as the twine became loser the logs left us at a faster rate. By the time we reached ½ to ¾ of a mile we had to abandoned ship. Each of us floating down the river scrapping our lower bodies on the rocks and river bottom while hanging onto the logs to keep our heads above water. All the while twisting and turning as we tried to maneuver the remnants of our raft to the safety of shore. It was every man for himself each of us hanging on to his own log and laughing like crazy. As I said the trip was semi successful; that is only because none of us drowned. I have since given up the raft building business for good.

Perhaps one other story that bears telling would be why I had and still have a fear of snakes that surprise or startle me. It was during the summer of this same year that I was playing with a couple of kids my age from the same camp. I don't know what prompted this boy to throw what I thought to be a rattlesnake at me when I wasn't looking and then yell "Buddy look up!" which is exactly what I did as that snake wrapped itself across my bare chest and around my neck. I screamed as though I had just been bitten. Once I realized it was a bull snake my next move was to pound the stuffing out of the culprit. Every time he would try to get away I would chase him down and beat him some more. Later I asked why on earth he did that and he admitted he knew I was going to beat the beans out of him but he thought it would be funny just to hear me scream. After that I never wanted to have any contact with snakes and have been somewhat successful. However, as a volunteer for the fire corps in Arizona, one of my many tasks was to answer snake calls. Volunteers would go to the residence of people who had a rattlesnake in their garage, patio, and yard or sometimes in their house. We would pick up the snake put it in a box and return it to the desert. Not at all my favorite part of the job. Every time I had a snake call my wife would chuckle because she knew how hard that part of the job was for me

By now it is safe to say we were no longer considered migrant workers, but farm hands or field workers. We were people who worked in the valley wherever we could get a job, but always living in Naches or Lower Naches. Still not very affluent, but getting by. I can't imagine how many times Mom had told Clancy and me over the years that if the state ever quit giving her money (aid for dependent children was something that she had acquired in Washington) to take care of us and pay for our food and clothes. We would have to go into foster care and be split up. I never really understood the threat of foster care. I did however understand that my brother and I were not going to ever be split up. Not if I had any control over it. It was later in my life when I realized that it was most likely the money that appeared to be the only bond we had with Mom. I know that she did care about us, but she had too many problems of her own to deal with. Mom didn't really neglect us physically, we were fed and clothed but emotionally we were just there. Looking back I can't recall a time that either of us had ever been told "I love you" from Mom or Dad. I know in their own way they did. However, it is those few simple words that parents use to convey that unconditional acceptance of their children. To reassure them, to let them know that they belong and are cared for. When we were young and Mom threaten our lives with the gun. I now prefer to believe that she wasn't really going to pull the trigger. It's easier to believe it was all brought about by frustration, alcohol and an illness. If you've never heard "I love you", you really don't miss it; at least not until you get to a point in your life when you learn to love; when someone in your life teaches you that it is ok to show emotion. When you realize that you are lovable. My dad taught me that Jesus loves us. I believed him then and I believe that now. But as a kid you can't help but wonder why can't my parents or some other person love me as well? It would be hard not to notice the difference in the interaction of some families compared to your own. That makes you start to wonder why the difference. Am I missing something here? I know as I grew older I asked myself many times what did I do wrong that no one wanted me. The answer to that question was "nothing". It just so happened that this was the circumstance I was in, these were the cards I was dealt. As Dad would say "pick up your bottom lip and quit feeling sorry for yourself"

This is also about the time I began to realize that we were poorer than most of my classmates. However, not everything was bad. Even being without a great deal of money there were happy times in our lives. Times when we went camping or fishing in some of the rivers or desert lakes along the Columbia Basin. Occasionally we would drive over the mountain to the coast and dig for clams or catch sea perch from the shore. I imagine there must have been a limit on how many clams or sea perch we were allowed. But to my brother and me it was entirely based on how many we could carry home. Dad had a brother that lived in Kelso, Washington, and we would stop to see him on the way. As far as I knew at that time it was his only relative. Uncle George was a great guy and I enjoyed every time we would see him. He always gave us money for a show and something to eat during the film. But he also genuinely seemed to like Clancy and me. It was a far better life for all of us since Dad had quit drinking and decided to follow the Lord; even if it often meant church 3-4 times a week.

Seventh and eighth grades found us back in Lower Naches again. I was doing ok in school, playing ball, chasing girls, and all the things I was supposed to be doing at that age. I rarely got into trouble at school and was becoming popular with my classmates, mostly because of my athletic ability. I played football, basketball and my favorite sport at that time baseball. I stood out as a fairly accomplished athlete for my age and was always playing up a year or two above my age bracket in sports. Unfortunately I wasn't pushed nearly as hard in the classroom by my teachers as I was on the field by my coaches. I played Little League Baseball in the summer like every other kid at that age. I pitched and played third base or short stop. I was selected to play on the little League All Star Team two years in a row.

I recall it was when I was in the seventh grade age 12 that Dad got a job thinning apples in the spring and I was going to help. I could work my school and ball schedule around my time in the field with him. This stands out in my mind because the farmer agreed to pay Dad $1.25 per hour and only give me $0.75. Dad told the guy "no my son works like a man and you can pay him like one." Probably one of the proudest moments working with Dad that I can ever remember. I worked hard that spring to make sure I wouldn't let him down. He would break for lunch and say "let's take a 20 minute nap." He would then lay his pocket watch on his chest and sleep for 20 minutes and wake up. I tried that once later in my life and woke up about 3 hours later.

Student body elections were held in the seventh grade for the officers who would be the governing body in the eighth grade. I was nominated for president and was elected. Our school had never had a school dance and my first undertaking as president was to convince the Student Body Counselor that we wanted and deserved the right to have a dance. After him we had to convince PTA. Unlike Mom when she went to the PTA meeting after the teacher hit me. I didn't go there to make an impression on the side of someone's head. But I did make an impression on the people at the meeting. We were granted our dance but only after they insisted that a dance studio in Yakima come out to our school and give about three months of lessons once each week. We learned to Waltz, Cha-Cha and Jitter Bug These lessons were paid for by the PTA. I was a hero with the girls and some of the boys, but I still couldn't dance very well. I was also on the newspaper staff and it was during one of our paper assembling events that a girl stole my stapler and I stole it back. Unfortunately for me she had older brothers and was proficient at fighting. She kicked me in the knee so hard that she knocked a bone tumor that was on the inside of my knee off. It would slide up and down my leg just under the skin and it needed to be removed. We were aware that it was there and would eventually need to come off. But not yet. I wanted to wait until after football season. I didn't get my way. I had surgery on my knee shortly after the kick. There were teachers, coaches and one very upset girl all wondering if it was cancer and would I be able to play again. While I was recovering at home Mom went to school to get my homework. The girl who kicked me came up to Mom crying like crazy and so sorry that it was her fault that my leg had been removed. According to Mom, she was almost hysterical blaming herself for my career ending amputation. Of course Mom knew nothing about the incident she was describing. I was at home, the tumor was benign, my leg was still attached and I would return to school in a few days. Mom explained all this to her and she felt much better before Mom left school. However, I got blamed for the entire story and for my cruelty to this poor young lady who had kicked me. I had nothing to do with any of it. My good friend and student body VP decided on his own to tell her my leg had been amputated and I would never walk again. Actually I was back working out with the football team within two weeks. My friend still thinks it was funny but then he didn't get in trouble like I did.

There were rules for being on the various teams I played on and I was aware of them. Unfortunately I violated every one of them. I started drinking and smoking between the 7th and 8th grades not every day but whenever I had the chance. I got caught by Dad once on a Saturday night. I came home from being out with friends. We were living on a farm at the time. The owner let us live in an old farm house that had several rooms, a wood stove for heating and cooking, water in the kitchen but of course that dreaded outhouse. This place had a bedroom upstairs for Clancy and me as well. The night I got caught I tripped on the stairs going up and fell. Dad came out to see what all the noise was and found me more than a little intoxicated. As I look back I'm sure it must have really hurt him to see me doing these things at such an early age. The very same things he had done in his life. As parents we want our children not to make the same mistakes and poor choices we made. Dad was probably afraid I would become what he once was. A former drunk or an alcoholic. More than anything he wanted me to be more like he was now. He wanted me to accept the Savior as he had and follow Christ throughout my life. But I wasn't heading in that direction. The next morning he came to wake me up for church as he always did and I refused to go. A few weeks prior to this day I had told my Sunday school teacher exactly where I thought she could go. Because of something she said that was clearly directed at me. She had very plainly stated that she didn't want boys like me in her class. I was angry and I believed that she was wrong. When I got up to leave she said to sit down and without thinking I told her exactly where to go and I walked out of Sunday School.

In Mark 2:17 (NIV) Jesus states that "It's not the healthy that need a doctor, but the sick. I didn't come to call the righteous, but sinners." Having me in her class; in church; is exactly what she should have wanted. Dad made me go back to the church and apologize to her for what I said. I believed then as I do now that she was wrong. The Bible states repeatedly that God wants and accepts those who are struggling and I was struggling. If she were alive today I would gladly apologize again for what I said because that was wrong of me. Only this time I would mean it.

The morning after I was caught drinking, Dad and I argued about that event, my drinking and several other things relating to the church. But I refused to go. This time Mom came to the rescue and finally made him quit whipping me. I was sorry for the things I said and the disrespectful way I was speaking to him. But I didn't want to back to that church.

I only argued with him one more time after that and that argument was the reason for the last whipping he ever gave me. I called him a liar. Dad took a dim view of that, and he started whipping me pretty good. This time I merely stood there and took it, no show of pain, no emotion, nothing. He had taught me most of my life that big boys don't cry and men don't cry either. In my opinion I had just crossed that threshold to the point where I was either a big boy or a man. I was tough and I had decided I wasn't going to ever cry again no matter what.

All of my emotions were locked up in a box. The emotions that most kids experience I had decided to never let them show. I had made the decision to put a lid on that box keep them there, and they would not emerge again for a very long time.

This was not only the last but probably the worst whipping I had ever received from Dad. I can only imagine that he was frustrated beyond belief. He was spanking me and I did not respond, I just stood there. And to top it all off his little boy had just called him a liar. He now had two boys who weren't exactly what one would expect or hope for; both headed down a road to destruction, following the same path he had followed in his younger years.

GUS

Dad used to tell a story about a dog he once had it was a Llewellyn setter. He said she was a great hunter and had a sharp nose. After some searching I found one and brought him home. I called him Gus. I had visions of Gus and me roaming the hills and orchards bringing home wild game of all varieties. Ducks, quail, pheasants and rabbits all of which I was becoming fairly proficient at shooting. It was going to be such fun, just a boy and his dog. Gus on the other hand had different ideas of what he could or should hunt. He could care less about all of the wild game I had envisioned for us. However, he did have a great nose for clean clothes. Gus would roam the area around our neighborhood and pull clothes from the various clothes lines dragging them through the hills and orchards, catching them on things and tearing them while dragging them through the mud. Mom took a dim view of this action when it was our clothes. The neighbors thought even less of it when it was theirs. I tried to break him of it; I even tied him up; but when he got free, the clothesline was fair game.

Then came a day that Dad said "we can't have this any longer. We can't afford to replace other people's clothing. You have to put him down." In our world that didn't mean going to the vet to be euthanized, or giving him to someone else so it would become their problem. It meant exactly what he said. I had to put Gus down just as you would a sick cow or a lame horse or a rabid dog.

I dug a hole and put Gus in the hole and while he looked up I emptied my 12 gauge shot gun; all three shots. As I buried Gus in that orchard there were still no tears. I had vowed never to cry again and I couldn't or wouldn't start now. It wasn't that I didn't feel just as strongly as other kids my age or that I didn't have emotions of sorrow and sadness. But, for me as I stated earlier it was a way of survival the only way I knew. Don't ever show weakness; someone will take advantage of it.

I don't want you to get the idea that Dad was cruel or mean because that is just not true. Yes we got some pretty hard thrashings mostly with a belt, a strap, a stick or his hand. However, in his defense he rarely hit us with a fist unless one of us did as I did with the finger in his face and I deserved that. I don't think he ever hit Clancy like that but he may have. I just wasn't aware of it. In all sincerity I deserved almost every whipping Dad gave me. I know I had a bit of an attitude and a quick response and a smart mouth. I knew I would get a whipping for talking back or making smart remarks, but I just didn't seem to care. This attitude was the reason for most of my discipline. But overall Dad was fair and fun to be around. You only had to be respectful, work hard and do your best at everything you attempted. His method of discipline wasn't meant to punish as much as it was intended to correct our behavior. But most of all it was intended to prepare us for the world that awaited us as fruit pickers or migrant workers. He knew it wouldn't be easy. It hadn't been easy for him, and he expected we would face the same situations. I really do appreciate him for who he was, as well as what he tried to do for me. Perhaps not then, but I do now. I inherited a good work ethic from him, one that I wasn't even aware of. I know now that as much as he wore out the seat of my pants he also wore out the knees of his pants. Dad prayed many times every day for my brother and me. He spent hours in prayer. It wasn't at all unusual to see Dad on his knees at any time of the day or night just praying silently. I wish he were alive today so I could thank him for that. I am convinced that his prayers for my life made a difference in what I am as a man today. It's not that I am anything great because I am not. However, it is more about what I would have been if he hadn't prayed for my life, and God had not let his Grace surround me.

In Daniel 9:23 (NIV) the angel Gabriel appeared to Daniel and said "the minute you started to pray an answer was given. In John 14: 14 Jesus stated that "You may ask for anything in my name and I will do it."

I am sure that is exactly what Dad was doing all of those hours he spent on his knees. He was asking for us. For our safety as well as our salvation.

I think it was the summer between my 7th grade and 8th grade years Dad found out about a seminary that the Pentecostal Church was going to hold in Puyallup Washington, He really wanted to go. The class would be held for 3 months during the summer. With Dad studying for seminary there was no income so Clancy and I worked that summer to support his efforts to become ordained as a minister of the Gospel. He never had his own church. I don't believe he even wanted one. However, he did preach and was referred to by most people as Reverend Salsbury. This was a proud moment for all of us. I am especially proud of him. Just imagine a man with a third grade education, an alcoholic, and a migrant worker. A man who almost beat a man to death and probably would have if others hadn't intervened. And yet God somehow got his attention in a peach tree. And now about 4 years later that person is an ordained minister. That's quite an accomplishment. It is utterly amazing what God can accomplish and the people he uses for his glory.

After we returned home from his time at seminary, I continued to pull away from the church and from God even more. I let people and peer pressure drive a wedge between me and the God who had gotten Dad's attention in that tree. The God that had so drastically changed his life as well ours. After all I had seen one would think I would have known better. However, having a Sunday school teacher tell me that I wasn't wanted or didn't belong in her class, and my encounter with what I will call the wayward evangelist gave me the excuse I was looking for to abandon the church and God altogether. It's easy to find an excuse if you're looking for one.

THE WAYWARD EVANGELIST

We never had a lot of material possessions but what we had Dad would share with anyone. He was extremely generous and felt that sharing was what Christ had commanded of us.

During this time in our church it wasn't unusual to have tent meetings or have an evangelist come to visit our church for a revival. Dad often had someone stay at our house even though it wasn't much, it was a place to sleep and it was accepted. One particular team of evangelists was made up of a Preacher, his wife who was a singer, an accordion player/singer and his friend, a piano player. They would come to town for a week and hold prayer meetings every night. They would stay with any family that would house them. On this particular occasion we had the accordion player/singer and his piano playing friend at our house.

It was summer and I was going to go to Naches a distance of about 7 miles. I had hitch hiked there many times. However, the accordion player offered me a ride and would let me drive his car there as well. So I took the offer. About half way there he ask me to stop for a second. I did and he pulled a very graphic, very vivid, pornographic magazine from under the seat and showed me the pictures.

I wasn't sure what to think. I had seen a lot but nothing quite like this. Then he decided to tell me what he had in mind for the two of us to do. I wasn't as innocent or naive as he had hoped. He failed to realize that being Clancy's younger brother I knew things way beyond my years. I hit him and got out of the car. When I returned home he was gone. He and his friend had decided to leave a little earlier than expected. I never told my dad of this incident for fear of what he would have done to that person who was supposedly a man of God. But I probably should have. What if I had been naïve? How many children could have been, or perhaps, were molested by this man, a man that everyone trusted, an evangelist singing and preaching the word of God?

I re-live this incident not to judge the man who attempted to molest a 12 year old, but to make the point that I let that event and other events in my life drive that wedge between me and God. At the point I let that happen I was no better than he was. Romans 3: 23 states that "all have sinned." Turning my back on God was a sin regardless of the justification I had in my mind. I blamed God for the acts of an individual and I was wrong.

It was years before I was able to return to worship the same God that my dad loved and had somehow gotten his attention that day in a peach tree. One thing I know for sure is that God doesn't have any grandkids. Because of the belief of your father you don't automatically get a free pass into heaven. It has to be a personal decision. The good news is though, that God's Grace is always there, always available to anyone. To people like my dad, myself, and yes even for people like the evangelist who was a pedophile.

Fortunately for all of us, God is patient as well as gracious. He never left my side even though I tried hard to turn my back on him. God never turned his back on me. I know it pained my dad to see me pulling away; just as it pains all parents when they see a child making a huge mistake and feel powerless to stop it. However, he continued to pray for me as well as my brother.

On a brighter note at this same time in my life Clancy and some of his friends decided to box for the YMCA. As you know by now I had been fighting with him since I was big enough to walk, so I signed on to box as well. I trained with kids bigger and older than I was. Boxing in a ring sounded like a great time to me; 16 oz. gloves, no head gear, but with gloves that big you can't really get hurt. Right? I did this along with all the other activities I was involved with and juggled my working, drinking and school schedule until basketball season in the eighth grade. I came to practice one day with a swollen eye and a fat lip from a fight that weekend. The coach got angry and told me to choose between basketball and boxing. Based on the condition of my face and how hard that last kid could hit; I chose basketball. I think it was a wise decision.

I continued, however, to stay gone on the weekends working on Saturdays and Sundays at whatever farm I could get a job. I was drinking in the evening, running around being stupid and trying to act cool. Our family seemed to be getting along pretty well but I sensed my parents had given up on trying to control my activities. I came and went as I pleased. From age twelve on I was required to pay board and room. However, with that I had the freedom to do just about anything I wanted. This seemed reasonable to me at the time. I believe my parents had finally given up on trying to control me, but Dad still prayed.

My own children have said on more than one occasion that as a parent I was far too strict with them. Without going into a great detail I have told them that I speak from experience when I say it is better to have a parent that is strict and cares about you than one who has no concern about what you do, where you are, if you are eating, sleeping, going to school, or any of the other things that normal parents find to worry about. I was not told to do homework except by a few teachers. Dad tried to maintain control of us but as we got older it just didn't seem to work. I imagine they could have turned us over to Social Services if there was one; but they didn't, and I'm thankful for that.

On two separate occasions when I was boxing, I thought I was pretty good so I challenged Dad to a fight. I can recall both fights in detail; every punch that was thrown is so etched in my memory it seems like only a short time ago that it happened. The first time I was still in 7th grade. I told Dad since I was taller than he was and even though he outweighed me I could take him. We weren't mad just going outside to fight at my request. There were no 16 oz. gloves and no headgear. We squared off I put my guard up and he hit me twice before I could take the first swing. Sitting on my butt I looked up and calmly told him that was good but I'll be back. A year later (8th grade) I returned. Same request same scenario except this time I swung once. I have no idea where he went but he certainly wasn't where I was swinging. He hit me twice. Again I was sitting on my butt in the yard looking up. I repeated my comment from the year before. "I'll be back."

When I started the ninth grade I had decided that playing football was going to be a problem. Rules were more stringent, kids were bigger but most of all this would require a change in my lifestyle. I wasn't sure I was big enough or good enough to play with the upper classmen. When I came home on the 1st day of school, Dad ask about practice. I informed him that I wasn't playing. Remember earlier when I mentioned that Dad said he wouldn't have a coward in the house, and he would repeat that to me later. This was that day. Dad told me to get out and not come back until I was playing on the freshman football team. Somehow; he knew I was afraid. Afraid that everyone around me had seem to have grown over the summer. Dad knew that I had been playing since I could walk and that I loved the game. He simply gave me a choice, that little push that I needed, go out for football or find another place to live. I was on the team the next day and I never regretted it. That team of freshmen only lost

1 game in 4 years of high school football. However, my dad never got to see me play a single game. Dad died on October 4th 1960, my freshman year. I never got to challenge him to that third fight either. This time I may have gotten to swing twice before he set me on my butt. But I know he would have set me there.

The morning Dad died he was scheduled to have a routine visit with his doctor. He had been plagued with a bad heart all of his life and had had several minor heart attacks over the years. This day was to be no more than a follow-up from a previous visit to see how he was doing.

I was getting ready for school when Dad called me into the kitchen shook my hand looked me in the eye and said " Goodbye Buddy take care of your Mom." I responded with the usual kid talk, "yeah no problem Dad; I'll see you tonight." I never dreamed at the time that this would be his last words to me, but I did think it odd to say goodbye since he was just going in for a check-up. He wasn't supposed to have to stay at the hospital or anything. Mom said he died in the car on the way to the doctor's office. He simply laid his head down in the seat and died. Perhaps some people know when their time is up, maybe he just felt that God had told him that he had done all he was expected to do on this earth. After all he had taken us from California before the flood. He had raised two grandkids the best he knew how and he had planted in our minds the "Grace of God." Whatever the case I am totally convinced that Dad knew he would die that day and that is why he shook my hand and said goodbye.

Dad died on a Tuesday and I played a game on Thursday evening in his honor. Some people felt I was being egotistical. Acting as though the team couldn't do without me, but that wasn't the case at all. It was because of him that I was playing and because of him I would continue to play. Even though I wanted to cry like any other kid would have. I didn't cry at Dad's funeral for two reasons. I was told that if I cried, Mom would lose it completely and as I said before I was beyond tears and men aren't supposed to cry. So I didn't. This was something that very few people understood at the time. Most relatives felt my lack of tears was a lack of gratitude for all my grandparents had done for me over the years. It was pointed out by more than one person that they took me in when no one else wanted me. Or as one person stated to me, "You just don't care about anything do you"? They were all wrong. I cared and I cared deeply, but I was overwhelmed and confused about what exactly was expected of me. I had just turned 14, my brother had left earlier that year, and Dad had left me with the task of "Buddy take care of your Mom". How was I going to do that, should I drop out of school and get a job? How would we get food, pay the rent and all the things associated with maintaining a house?

Since Dad had died and was no longer working on that farm, the owners of the house wanted us out as soon as we could leave. Mom found a small place just outside of Naches and we moved in.

I can only assume Mom must have received some form of a welfare check after pop died as well as the ADC she received for me. I worked and gave Mom most of my earnings. I continued playing ball and going to school when it was convenient, and of course I was still drinking as often as I had the chance.

Without Dad in our life there was even less control of me and of the things I was doing. Mom quit going to church completely and reverted back to the drinking habits she had when I was younger, and with that came depression and talks of suicide. However, she no longer threatened me or pointed a gun at me as she had done when I was younger. I believe she knew she wouldn't do it anyway, and besides, I was the one working and adding to the family income. Before, when I wanted to get something to drink as a minor it was difficult but not at all impossible. If you knew where to go and what to look for you could get beer, wine or whiskey on most Friday nights and for sure on Saturday nights. No one ever locked their cars and most drunks would buy whatever alcohol they wanted for the weekend before they went to the bars and put it in their cars. We would simply go behind the bars where the cars were parked and help ourselves.

After Dad died it was easier for me to get alcohol, I just ask Mom and gave her either money or some of the beer we bought and she supplied the alcohol whenever I wanted it. Once in a while she would insist that if I were going to drink I needed to do it at the house. However, she soon realized she couldn't enforce that so she quit trying. I continued to play ball all the while managing not to get caught breaking training rules. As a freshman I played football, (quarterback and defensive back), basketball (point guard), track (pole vault and the 440). I gave up baseball completely although it was probably my best sport. I really wanted to learn to play basketball. I had seen the Globe Trotters and was amazed at what they could do with a ball. I figured with enough practice I could do some of the same things. I practiced every chance I got learning to dribble between my legs as well as dribble and pass accurately behind my back. This was something that just wasn't done in regular American basketball except by Bob Cousy a professional player for the Boston Celtics. And of course the Trotters who were my heroes. However, at this point basketball was by far my worst sport. So much so that after my freshman season it was suggested by a coach that I may like wrestling better. I worked all year to bring my basketball skill level up to a place where I could be considered a decent ball handler and basketball player. I practiced every spare moment that I had. During this time I had no idea how Mom and I were going to live and where we would get money even for the basics. But we managed. I worked when I could, I drank more than I should and still practiced basketball as much as time would allow. It must have worked, my practice paid off. My sophomore year I was the only sophomore asked to play on the varsity basketball team. I find that amusing when only a year earlier I was asked if wrestling would be a better sport for me to pursue.

My freshman year would not be complete without the telling of this last incident. And again the Grace of God in my life.

I had discovered girls earlier in school (6th grade) but until my freshman year I had honestly never had a real girlfriend. A friend of mine from football and I would double date. He was a junior and could drive. We had established a tradition of racing the twenty or so miles to the town where his girlfriend lived. Timing ourselves to see how fast we could maneuver the roads in his Dad's 1955 Ford Crown Victoria. According to the police report we were doing between 65 and 70 MPH when we left the road. I know that just before we started down the hill toward the stop sign at the end of the road, he said we had just hit 120MPH. If you were to remember, I stated earlier that there were several incidents in my life "that only God could have helped me through"; this has to be one of them.

At the bottom of this hill was a stop sign. It meant to stop. You could only go left or right. There was no road straight ahead only mailboxes and a ditch about 20 ft. wide. He and I went straight. As we were sliding through the intersection and across the road. I could hear His voice and it is with me still. "We aren't going to make it Bud ". I responded with a simple "yep". I watched as everything seemed to take place in slow motion. The mailboxes hit the front fender and one came right at the window on my side but didn't hit it. Instead it bounced off of the hood and I watched it slowly go by the passenger side window. It should have hit directly where I was sitting, but it didn't. The car then slammed into the bank on the far side of the ditch. My friend and driver was hanging on to the steering wheel so tight and hard that he bent it forward 90 degrees. He literally bent the steering wheel in half. His right leg came up from the floor and hit the dash with such force that his leg put a dent in the dash that looked as though some one had hit it with a sledge hammer. We have no idea how they came off of his head, but his glasses were found lying in the back window. After the mail box went by my window and we hit the bank the sudden stop of momentum caused my head to hit the dash with such force that I put a huge dent in the dash similar to the one he had made with his leg. My head then bounced up and went partially through the front window of the car, breaking out the window and sending glass everywhere. My left leg went forward striking the dash just as his right leg had done. Now the dash had three very large dents. One from each of our legs and one from my head. Amazingly we both stepped out of the car basically unhurt. I had a cut on the back of my head where it had hit the window and a knot on my forehead where I had hit the dash. He had a bump on his right leg and I had one on my left leg. But imagine this! No seat belts! No air bags! Somewhere between 65 and 70 MPH head on into an immovable object, and we both walked away unhurt. Fortunately there was no one else was in the car when we crashed. Later we both had to appear in court where the judge took us into his chambers. Just the 3 of us. He was very well versed in telling us how dumb we were in our race against the clock. He made us go through a photo album he kept in his chambers. Pictures of kids who didn't make it. Teenagers who had done less damage to their car, and were going at a much slower speed than we were at the time of the accident. Kids who lost their lives because of one stupid decision. His last words to us were simple. "You two should be dead. You just don't realize it. "I realize it now. It is simple. There are some things in life that only God can get you through. When this story was related to a writing class I was taking a student looked at me and said "boy you were lucky" without thinking I replied "no I have to disagree with you. I wasn't lucky" He looked at me with a surprised quizzical look. I went on to say "I wasn't lucky I was protected; as

I said before there are times and circumstances that only God can get you through."

I managed to get through my freshman year and I didn't fail any classes. I should have probably failed a couple, but they were taught by coaches. I found out from the coach that if I failed I wouldn't be able to play football my sophomore year. Both coaches gave me a D and I had to promise to do better next year. As a sophomore I was playing Jr. Varsity and Varsity football along with several other sophomores from my class. I mostly hung out with the juniors and seniors and on one particular evening prior to homecoming, we had our usual bonfire, cheerleading, fight songs, and all things associated with a high school football homecoming. I'm not sure who came up with the idea but we were going to play our rival Highland High School. Highland had built a new school about five years previous with a large sweeping lawn in front of the school and a hedge in the shape of a large "H". The idea was to cut the middle out of the H and stack the cut limbs to form a large "N" for Naches High School. It seemed innocent enough and we would have gotten away with it if the student body VP hadn't admitted his involvement and gave the names of everyone else that was involved except his younger brother. The picture of the hedge made the local news. Nine of the eleven starters for the homecoming game were involved. We all had to go before their principal and stand before the entire Highland High School Student Body and apologize for cutting their hedge. Our principal informed me along with the rest of the team that I was the only person involved who he could imagine doing something so criminal as that act of vandalism. At this point I hadn't really done anything to him that should have triggered a statement like that, but the line was drawn; he didn't like me and he said as much. Our coach was furious. However, not at what we did because he admitted to several of us it was the funniest thing he had seen happen in years, he was angry that one of our teammates not only admitted he was involved but gave the names of his teammates that were involved also. Later that same year the coach arranged a grudge match between myself and the team mate who turned us all in. He was the student Body VP and we would box at the annual boxing event our school held to raise money for the football program. He was a senior and I a sophomore He was at 6 ft. and 170 and I at 5ft. 8 in. and probably 150 at that time. I won that fight but lost the war. I was kicked out of school the following Monday. It was true I had been drinking and when asked, I admitted it. The principal had told me previously, on more than one occasion, that my family was just no good. He also told me that I had no business being with decent kids in his school. I gave him the reason he was looking for. My punishment was suspension. I could not participate in track or on any other athletic team or any extracurricular event the rest of my sophomore year. My junior year I was also to be prohibited from playing football as well. The coach and I argued with the principal that I was between sports at the time of the incident and not breaking any athletic commitment. However, as stated earlier the principal had taken a real dislike to me, but the coach was very persuasive and it was finally agreed that I could play football as a junior but nothing the rest of my sophomore year. Up until this point, I had been pretty good at obeying the training rules during season not breaking the rules or code of conduct for athletes at least not often. I will admit there were times during football that I would do things I knew were wrong. Basketball however was a different story. As I said, I was the only sophomore on the Varsity and I didn't want to take a chance on losing that status. Athletics was the only thing I had to keep me on track and attending school on a routine basis. I attended class so I could practice. I played 3 quarters of Junior Varsity and then would suit up for the varsity game where I was only allowed 1 quarter because of league rules. I could have just played Varsity but I knew as a sophomore there would be too much bench time and I wanted to play. This was the perfect solution as far as I was concerned. I was able to practice with both teams and got a lot of playing time.

I need to go back briefly to my freshman year. Six months after Dad died Mom remarried. She married Gene Reandeau. He was a nice enough guy, a mechanic by trade. She said she was lonely and wanted to marry. I told her I really didn't care if she married. I was living my life and she hers. I guess what I wasn't prepared for was to learn that she and Gene were going to leave and move to Nebraska sometime shortly after they were married. They made this move during the spring of my sophomore year right after my suspension. I stayed in Washington, rented a house, attended school and worked the fields whenever I could. When the principal had taken away my participation in athletics, he also took away the only thing keeping me in school. I essentially quit attending the last semester. I did manage to pass all of my classes with a little help. However, the principal was definitely out to remove me from "his school" as he had put it.

It didn't take long for me to fulfill the principal's plan for my future. Leaving a 15 year old boy alone to fend for himself is certainly a path to disaster and I took that path.

Each fall we had a dance to kick off the school year. It was the beginning of my junior year. I was the starting quarterback on a team that had never lost a game and I wasn't about to blow my chance to play for the next two years. I worked hard and I was committed to follow the rules laid out by the coaches. That team went on to win the state title my senior year but I wasn't part of it.

This particular dance turned out to be my last activity at Naches High School. I went to the dance had a good time and never gave a thought that I was being scrutinized or that I may have done something wrong. I had not been drinking prior to the dance, or at the dance. However, I was with one of my friends who was drinking. "Guilt by association"; is the term he used. And the principal got his wish. I was soon to be history and someone else would be the starting QB. The choice he gave me was very simple because he knew I was living alone. I could either go to Nebraska and live with my mom and Gene, or he would see to it that I ended up in jail. Even though I had done nothing wrong, the decision was final; the coach couldn't help me this time. I chose to go to Nebraska. The coach and I sat down and we talked at length about the new opportunities I would have in Nebraska. How I could use this time to find new friends that weren't quite so likely to lead me down that path of self-destruction that I seemed to be headed. I don't think he had ever been to Nebraska or he may not have been so agreeable that I go.

A week before I was removed from school my junior history teacher and varsity basketball coach gave a lecture to the class about the results of a test we had participated in as sophomores'. He went into detail about students that were performing way below their ability. He made it very clear that whoever these students were it was about to change. He was going to personally see to it that they were held accountable for their effort and grades. Like most of the students in the class I sat there wondering what got him all excited and who could he be referring to. I found out when I went to say goodbye to a coach that I respected. He asked me if I had any idea who he was talking to during that lecture and I honestly told him I had not a clue. He informed me that I had the second highest scores in my class on the test we had taken during our sophomore year and yet my grades were horrible. Perhaps the worst waste he had ever seen during his teaching career. He was sorry I was leaving, but encouraged me to use the brain God had given me and to try hard to turn my life around when I got to Nebraska.

Gene's married daughter and Mom drove out from Nebraska to pick me up and take me to their house; a trailer in the very far Southwest corner of Nebraska. A place where Nebraska, Colorado and Kansas all touch.

IMPERIAL NEBRASKA

It would be hard to explain what I felt. I was going someplace completely foreign to me. I was a little scared and anxious, not really knowing what to expect. I would be living with Mom and her husband. Who in reality would actually be my step grandfather but I always called him Gene. He and Mom had left me in Washington when they moved earlier that year. Therefore, I think it would be fair to say they weren't all that excited about the idea of me living with them in Nebraska either. But they did come to get me.

Dad always claimed to have itchy feet that's why we moved so much. So I had lived in a lot of places and one more should be a walk in the park. I had two years of school to finish if I chose, or I could just walk away and hitch-hike back to Naches. Knowing I wouldn't be allowed to go to school in Naches or play ball helped me make the decision to give Nebraska a chance.

I can understand that I may have been a bit of a problem for some people while living by myself in Naches. However, I felt I had done quite well all things considered. I hadn't been arrested or gone to jail. Naches was where I wanted to live, and I was sure that I would return someday. It was still where I called home. I didn't like anything I had seen in Nebraska during the few days I was there before starting school. I had lived in the Naches area longer than anywhere in my short life. It was a town tucked up in the foothills leading to the

Cascade Mountains and Mount Rainier, Mount Adams, Mount Hood and all the other mountains of the Cascades. Naches was a place where rivers were clear and ran swiftly out of those mountains. Trout were abundant and as a kid I brought more than my share home for dinner. I wandered in those hills and knew some of them as well as anyone. The Yakima Valley was noted for its apples, peaches, cherries, pears and many other fruit crops that grew abundantly in the valley. These were the things I had grown up harvesting things I understood. Except for a couple of months during the winter. The valley was always green.

In the southwest corner of Nebraska you can find Imperial Nebraska. Imperial is the county seat of Chase County and as such was the largest town in the county. Imperial boasted a population of approximately 1200 people and home to the high school I had decided to attend. Chase County High School home of the Longhorns. I was going to transition from Blue and Gold Naches Rangers to Black and Orange Imperial Longhorns "a cow for a mascot." At that time there were just under 3000 people in the entire county. You could stand on the hood of your car and see for miles in every direction (there weren't any hills). They raised corn, wheat, and cows. I knew nothing about any of those crops or how you picked them. The crops from the summer had been harvested and everything as far as I could see was brown, barren and dirty. My opinion was that nothing could have been worse than this place and spending the next two years with mom and Gene. However, I had told myself I was going to try and clean up my act. I was committed to try and do just that.

After watching the Longhorns play football on Friday night I decided that I would enroll on Monday and see if I was going to be able to play for Chase County. I felt that I was as good as and perhaps even better than the existing quarterback. I'm not being boastful just honest. If the teachers and coaches told me that I wouldn't be able play I was going hitchhike back to Washington as fast as I could. However, the Imperial coach called my coach from Naches. They involved both principles as well as the superintendents of both schools. Somehow even though I didn't have all of the credits required in Nebraska for a transfer student to play. The two coaches convinced everyone else to work it out. I was practicing Monday night. Compared to the football program I had just left, the Longhorns were more than a little lacking in depth and skill. There was no program to get the younger grade school kids ready for high school football. Their first introduction to football would be in the 9th grade. I had started playing organized school football in the 6th grade and most of my classmates started in the 7th and 8th grades at the latest. By the time we reached high school we knew all of the formations and plays we would use for the next 4 years. To me it seemed little wonder Imperial had lost 22 consecutive games. That amounts to two seasons without a win and they were playing their third game of the third losing season on Friday and weren't expect to win that game either. If I had known that, and had done my homework before enrolling in school I probably would have chosen Wauneta High School, about 18 miles away. Because of where Gene and Mom lived I could have gone to either school. But I was stuck here now and it was too late to transfer.

THE FIRST WEEK AND MY FIRST GAME IN IMPERIAL

There is no way to explain how different I was from kids in Southwest Nebraska. But I was different. I was different in the way I dressed, combed my hair and my attitude toward people in general. I imagine it was a combination of these things that made the coach decide to call me "Chicago". It also may have been my attitude that first day in school. The principal and I sat down in his office to decide which classes he thought I should take. Probably because of my previous test scores from Washington his choice for a science class was physics. It was the first class that I walked into in my new school. After all the usual introductions and the embarrassment of disrupting the class, I settled in to listen to the day's lesson. I remember they were talking about the universe and how far away some planet was from earth. Several students gave their opinion when the teacher said "let's ask the new kid. What do you think?" As always I had an answer. I simply said "I think I'm in the wrong class", and I got up and walked out and went back to the principal's office. Strangely enough later in my life physics became my favorite subject and I used those principles daily in my career. Whatever the coach's reason for calling me that name was known only to him and I really didn't care. I just wanted to play, be left alone, and eventually go back to Washington. I may not remember exactly or have recorded all of the details of the following story but I think with the included article from the Imperial Republic Newspaper and what I remember there is enough for you to understand and enjoy the strange happenings of my first week and my first game in another new school.

Imperial hadn't won a game in a very long time, and if success builds success then defeat can bring about defeat just as easily. Once a ship is in motion it's hard to turn it around. I had been in school 1 week and had only practiced 4 days and yet I started in Friday night's game on the special teams. In Washington I was the quarterback and defensive halfback or a free safety. We were playing Bird City, Kansas. I would be starting on special teams, defensive linebacker, and for a very few plays I would play halfback or quarterback. But, I was not given the freedom to throw the ball only hand the ball to someone else as he attempted to go through the line. During one particular set of plays, Bird City had the ball and I had positioned myself as the strong side linebacker. I was where I felt I should be based on my analysis of the situation on the field. Before Bird City came out of the huddle I heard this person on the sidelines yelling "hey 22 move over they're coming through here." My number was 22, but I had no idea who this fat guy with a clip board was. I had only been at the school 5 days and I hadn't seen this guy before. Therefore, I ignored him completely. The play developed and the runner came through the hole in the line just as the fat guy predicted. A couple of plays later I heard it again "hey 22 move over they're coming through here" I was pretty sure he couldn't be a coach. Surely I would have seen him at practice even if he was the freshman coach. Besides what gave him the right to tell me how to play my position. I knew better than to listen to some spectator on the sidelines. You just don't do that. Again I ignored him, and again they came right through the hole as he had predicted. A couple of plays later I heard the same voice "hey 22'. I didn't know who this fat guy was but obviously he had some knowledge of this particular team or of football in general that I didn't possess. I turned to him on the sideline and said "where are they coming this time. " I adjusted my position accordingly. He was right again and every time I heard "hey 22" I listened and would adjust as he suggested. The guy knew his football. During most of the game both teams were struggling very hard to see who could lose the game; rather than win. The game remained a stalemate until almost the very end, (0-0). As stated earlier we were playing Bird City Kansas their team not much better than ours only bigger. They had made an offensive drive and were threatening to score with a 1st and goal with only minutes left. I have no idea what got in to me; but I got mad at the situation we were in. We were about to lose the first game I was to be a part of in this awful place. (Remember my Washington team only lost one game in four years and as a freshman and sophomore we lost none). I didn't want to start my season here as part of a losing team. It was time to turn it around. I had been the quarterback in Washington, a team leader on offense as well as defense. Maybe it was just frustration about everything in my life to this point. The team, my move to Nebraska, getting kicked out of school in Washington, I really don't know what triggered it. But from my linebacker position I started yelling encouragement to a defensive line I didn't know. I don't think I knew more than 3-4 players' by name on the entire team. Whatever it was and whatever I said; it worked. Imperial dug in and held Bird City on 4th and goal from about the two yard line and the ball was turned over to us with less than two minutes left in the game. My thought was great a tie is better than a loss. Our coach called time out and in the huddle told me to play quarterback and throw the ball. (I recently contacted the Imperial Newspaper and obtained a copy of the article with their description of the last 2 minutes of the game) it's included. It is 2 minutes that I remember well as does almost everyone else who was on the field or in the stands that night. In all the football I have played or watched I have never seen a two minute drill quite like the one of that night. Unfortunately the article doesn't relate things such as me only being in school for 5 days and practicing for only 4. It merely states that I was a new addition to the team. Nowhere does it mentioned that the coach had me playing defense all evening with very little offensive playing time before those final minutes. Most people involved with the game still remember the outcome and each probably their own recollection of how we got there, and who did what. This is what I recall of the last two minutes. My version is pretty much in agreement with the newspaper.

I looked at the clock and it registered 1 minute and 45 seconds left and we have the ball on the wrong end of the field. The coach didn't give me a play to run he just said "throw the ball". I didn't know the name of the play I wanted to run. I simply gave the team these very basic directions. A standard play that every running back and end that has ever played the game knows how to run. "Ends go down to the linebackers and out then turn and go down field. Halfback angle across the middle. It worked as predicted their linebacker stayed with our ends and the halfback was open in the middle. He was brought down at about the 50 yard line. The next play it was the end who was open for a touchdown pass Thanks to a well called time out there were only a few seconds off the clock. We didn't convert the extra point, but we were up 6-0. Our team was ecstatic. We kicked off and Bird City failed to get outside the 10 yard line. We got the ball back and the coach didn't tell me what to do. I figured no one would ever expect me to pass again. The normal play would have been to take a knee and let the clock run out or just hand it to a running back. But I wanted to show the coach that he was wrong not letting me throw the ball for almost an entire game. I also wanted to make an impression to show the other players that I was good enough to play on their team, even if I wasn't a local. So I called the same exact play and received the same results; touchdown Imperial. We didn't get the extra point this time either. Again we kicked off and Bird City ran only one play when we intercepted a pass and was tackled somewhere close to mid field. From my perspective we were up 12 -0 and I should have just held onto the ball. But I didn't. Even if we lost the ball there was no chance of them catching us. So I called another pass play. Bird City was calling time out after each play and the clock was definitely in our favor. The stats at the end of the game looked something like this. With only 1 minute and 45 seconds left on the clock I managed to throw 4 or 5 passes (I'm not positive but I was told it was 5) for three touchdowns. Imperial won for the first time in 23 games 19-0. Prior to this night I had not managed to make a single friend in that town. But, on this particular Friday night; I was a hero. In that short 2 minutes of playing time. I had won the respect and favor of Imperial, Nebraska. I had made the impression I wanted. Cheerleaders were going crazy, people I had never seen before shaking my hand and slapping me on the back, girls who hadn't said a word to me all week suddenly couldn't resist telling me how happy they were that I had come to their school and giving me hugs. Overall, not a bad way to break in to a new school. I wasn't going to have to fight my way into school this time. However, I really didn't care. I just wanted to play ball and to be left alone. That was the third game of the season there were seven games left and we won 6 of the remaining 7. I believe I led the league in passing and was selected all conference even though I had missed the first two games. I was never able to repeat the performance of that first game. However, I did have some pretty good games during the rest of that season. The article from the paper is inserted below.

Longhorns Break Extended Jinx With Spectacular Victory Here Last Friday

Football fans in the Imperial area experienced a sensational break-through last Friday evening when the fired up Longhorns garnered their first victory in twenty-two tries. This represented two and one-half years of competition, and there was near pandemonium when the Longhorns finally started to "click".

And, while they were in the process the boys put on an exhibition of rapid scoring which would test the ability of a real professional squad, when they downed the Cardinals of Bird City, Kansas by a score of 19 to 6.

Although the Bird City lads were not as strong as some of the teams played this year, they out-weighed the Longhorns both in the backfield and on the line. With the past record of the local team the odds were not in their favor, but the CCHS were determined to turn them to their favor.

Almost as exciting as the victory itself was the flurry of scoring which the Longhorns demonstrated in the final two minutes of the contest. The game had been a see-saw affair all the way with no scoring until the final two minutes. Fans were beginning to see prospects of at least a tie game (0-0) which would be better than the losses of the past, when things began to happen.

In the statistics department the Longhorns were impressive by rushing 148 yards and passing 119 yards to 107 net yards. They lost 46 yards which means they gained 221 total yards. The Longhorns, via John Needham's strong right foot, averaged 49 yards per punt, and obtained 10 first downs as compared to the five Bird City gained. The Cardinal's 183 weight average in the line and the 159 pound average in the backfield out-weighed the Longhorns by 22 and 13 pounds respectively.

The first three quarters saw each team threaten a touchdown several times, but meet a strong defense each time. These quarters were filled with exciting scores.

The fourth quarter seemed to be going in the same manner as the first three, until there were about two minutes left in the game, then WHAM! it was at this time that Bud Salsbury, a newly added member to the (continued on page 8)

Longhorns Win . . .

(continued from page 1)

team, found Mike McNair on a pass play that covered approximately 50 yards. On the next play Bud again spotted Mike and hit him with a pass which meant six points. The PAT attempt by Neil Fortkamp failed.

The spirited Longhorns then kicked off to the Cardinals. After a booming "boot", John Needham caught the receiver on the three yard line. After holding them for four downs, the Longhorns gained possession again. This time the air route connected Salsbury to Dan Wallin for another six points. Again, the PAT attempt by Neil Fortkamp failed.

As before the Longhorns kicked off to the Cardinals, who passed on the first play from scrimmage, only to see it hauled in by Paul Thomas. Again Salsbury took to the air route, this time finding Marv Draper to his liking, for another six points. Neil Fortkamp then scored a "first" by kicking his first extra point. As the Longhorns kicked off, time ran out, leaving the score at 19-0.

Next week the Longhorns travel to the field of their perennial rivals Wauneta, boasting a posting a record identical to that of the Longhorns. If past records are any indication of the future, the two teams are evenly matched.

The probable starting line ups of the two teams, along with the weights are:

Wauneta

Jerry Sutherland, center, 157.
Kenny Smith, guard, 153.
Doug Resler, guard, 153.
Bob Janes, tackle, 212.
Ron Prior, tackle, 185.
Larry Kitt, end, 135.
Vaughn McBride, end, 166.
Keith Buffington, back, 140.
Duane Egle, back, 140.
Fred Baldonado, back, 140.
Larry Fanning, back, 158

C.C.H.S.

Terry McNair center 145; or Donnie Leach, 150.
Neil Fortkamp, guard, 161
Dan Wallin, guard, 160; or John Needham, 160.
Kent Molzahn, tackle, 235.
Mark Berry, tackle, 170.
Mike McNair, end, 160.
Dave Oltman, end, 150; or Bob Colson, 140.
Bud Salsbury, back, 150; or Rod Ashmore, 135.
Larry Newman, back, 135.
Paul Thomas, back, 140.
Marv Draper, back, 160.

Weight Averages

Wauneta

Backs—143 pounds
Line—168 pounds

Imperial

Backs—146 pounds
Line—161 pounds.

JT

It was important to me and I wanted to learn more about guy with the clip board? He obviously knew more about football than I did. Who was he? Why was he telling me how to play my position? The coach informed me he was Jim Cullen (JT) to his friends. He managed the local hardware store and enjoyed being able to contribute to high school football by keeping the statistics. He kept track of tackles, yards rushing, yards passing, and anything else the coach wanted to keep track of. I didn't know it at the time but this man would become my friend, my mentor, my boss and a father figure, a person for me to look up to. Jim was a person that would influence the rest of my life. In ways that neither of us ever would have expected. He and his wife Suzie had 7 children being a very devout Irish Catholic family. This was at a time when birth control was either not allowed or frowned upon. At the end of basketball season my junior year Jim gave me a job working in the hardware store that he managed. I could work before school, after practices, and on Saturdays. It was a steady income something I had never had in my life. When school ended that year he and Suzie asked me to stay with them in town so it would be easier to get to work. I could stay at their place as often as I wished sleeping in their basement. I could also stay at Mom and Gene's house if I chose at any time. I loved every minute at their house and their kids loved me. I baby sat for their 7 children and I was like a big brother to them all. Mom and Gene would frequently pop into town get a few dollars from me and then disappear again until the next time they needed some extra cash. Quite honestly working only part time I probably earned close to as much and maybe even more than Gene did on any given week especially during the winter. Somehow it seemed appropriate and I didn't mind helping them financially on occasion.

Before I go forward to basketball season at Imperial there is a funny story involving myself Jim and my first day on the job at the local hardware store in the spring of 1963.

I was to show up for my first day of work on a Saturday. Cullen gave me all of the basics I would need to do the jobs he wanted me to accomplish during the coming spring and summer, stock shelves, sweep the floor, basically any menial task that need done. I was also told to unload trucks and the railroad cars that brought lumber and other building products to town. Additionally, I was going to deliver goods to the local farmers and builders in the area. The store sold lumber, furniture, hardware and appliances as well as some sporting goods. But Jim was adamant about one thing. He was not to be interrupted if he were with a customer. He told me that I was to wait until he had finished before I spoke to him. Whatever it was he was sure it could wait. Jim was a salesman of extra ordinary talent, as you will soon discover, and that meant that when he was engaged in conversation it lasted for a lengthy period of time.

To start the day I came in late I had spent the night before someplace other than his house or Mom and Gene's and just over slept; embarrassing to say the least for the first day on the job. The store owned a 1 ton GMC pickup with a wooden box and bed that we used for delivery of small loads throughout the community. Jim ask me to rake all of the dead grass on our property. Then load it into the pickup and take it to the dump about 5 miles out of town. No problem, I spent all day raking and loading and sweeping and loading and eventually I was done and headed for the dump.

There was a lot of speculation about how this happened. Some say it was the exhaust pipe that caught the dead grass on fire. Others believed it was a spark under the ashes where I had chosen to dump the dead grass, and yet some people accused me of maybe having a smoke and flipping a cigarette into the grass. I wasn't smoking that day so I know that is not an option. Whatever it was I had raked some grass out of the truck and had turned my back to retrieve another tool. When I turned around there was a wall of fire coming at me from the back of the truck. I tried in vain to push the grass out and get the flames away from the cab and from myself. I was concerned about the location of the gas tank. I had visions of this thing going boom and wiping me and the truck out with a single bang. I was unsuccessful in my attempts to push the flame and the remaining grass from the bed of the truck. Eventually I had to scramble over the top of the cab and down the hood to the ground to escape the flames engulfing the bed of the truck.

There was one other man at the dump that day. He was unloading his garbage and when I asked for help he said as soon as he got done unloading he would give me a ride to town. I don't think I need to explain what my thoughts were of him at that moment. He certainly wasn't as excited about the truck burning up as I was. Someone in town must have seen the smoke and alerted the fire department. As we were headed into town they were heading out of town to the dump. I went into the store to tell Jim what was going on but he was with a lady customer. I remembered what he had said about not interrupting. So I just stood there, waiting for him to finish. I was shifting from foot to foot obviously concerned about something. Finally Jim got irritated so he ask 'what do you want'. I mumbled very quietly and quickly "trucks on fire" my head down my eyes looking at the floor. He asked again "what do you need' again I repeated the same words in the same manner "truck's on fire " Jim was getting angry so this time he said it very loud "Salsbury what do you want." This time he heard me, I looked at him and said "Jim the truck is at the dump and it is on fire". I had his attention.

All of the wood from the bed and the box had burned. But the volunteer firemen had gotten there in time to save the truck. One of the guys who worked at the store and I replaced all of the wood and made it even better than it was before. I didn't lose my job that day even though I probably should have. After all, on my first day at a new job I was late and burned up the entire bed of the truck. Instead of firing me, Jim choose to tell the story to anyone who would listen anytime the opportunity presented itself. For years after that first day Jim would tease me and the fire got bigger and the story got better. Later in life he loved to tell my children about their Dad's first day on the job. To my children Jim became Grandpa Jim and his wife Grandma Suzie.

That same year Jim and Suzie ask me to go on vacation with them to Minnesota. I accepted the invitation as the traveling baby sitter. This would allow Jim and Suzie to have time together. The kids loved the idea and we were off for a 10 day trip driving from Nebraska to Minnesota with 8 kids (counting me) and the two of them. All ten of us in a station wagon. During the day Jim and I went fishing and to see the Minnesota Twins play the Yankees. I was mesmerized the entire time we were at the stadium. At night I would baby sit for the children. They were a great bunch of kids. Jim and Suzie and the kids will reappear many times in my life and I will forever be indebted to them for all they did for me.

Now about the 1962-63 Basketball season in Imperial Nebraska.

For everything Imperial lacked in football it made up for in Basketball. I have no idea what type of record the Longhorn hoopsters had prior to my first season and it doesn't really matter for the telling of this story. Our starting five for that season were two seniors, two sophomores and myself as the only junior and the point guard. The play maker, the one who does the majority of dribbling and passing. That's what I did. I had practiced hard to be like Cousy or the Globe Trotters and I loved it. To me there is very little in sports as beautiful a well-executed play in a basketball game. In those days basketball was a non –contact sport and a foul was called for anything that even remotely looked like pushing or palming the ball. Today's basketball stars would have fouled out in the first five minutes of a game in the early 1960s. There was no shot clock and no three point shots at that time either.

We won a large majority of our games losing just a few. We won the South Platt Valley Tournament for the first time in what I was told to be 20 years. The local dentist stated that if we would win this tournament he would check and fix the teeth of each member of the team at no charge. I have no idea why he wanted to do that. I imagine being the only dentist in town he knew the condition of everyone's teeth. However, I seriously doubt he knew that I hadn't been to a dentist but maybe once or twice in my entire life. A souvenir from Dr. T that I still have today from that visit to him is a gold crown. Good to his word he paid for it and good to my word I took care of it and I still have it almost 60 years later.

A requirement of being on the basketball team was to dress for every game in a black suit, white shirt, black tie, and black shoes. A trench coat or rain coat was optional but the entire team was to look alike whenever or wherever we traveled. We were to always look and conduct ourselves as gentlemen. I'm not sure who put the word out that I could never afford something like that, but someone must have because a local fan and prominent business person decided that I needed a suit and they were going to help. I was told that an anonymous person in town wanted to give me a suit as a gift. I was taken by the coach to a local seamstress and measured for a suit. I have no idea who actually made the suit but before the season started, I was wearing a tailor made suit that met all of the dress requirements courtesy of a local fan. I eventually found out who the person was that paid for my suit even though it was a long time after graduation. I call them on occasion just to say hello. That suit cost $100.00 in 1962. I wore it for the next two years for every sporting event or dance that a suit was required.

There is one other person in Imperial who should be mentioned before I move forward with my story. Our music and drama teacher Mrs. McBride. When I registered in school that first day. I didn't know what classes to take, but I didn't want to take anything that would require too much work. One of the classes recommended to me was Choir (no homework). I can remember very well walking into that class on my first day of music and seeing Mrs. McBride standing before the class. She had to be the most beautiful lady I had ever seen. Her husband Lynn was the assistant coach for football and basketball. Over time I got to know them both very well. They had a love for children and education and they truly cared about each student. To them I wasn't just another voice in the choir or another number on the field. As I spent more time getting to know them in and out of the classroom, I realized, I would have done just about anything that Janie (Mrs. McBride to the rest of the class) ask of me. So when she suggested later that year that I take a part in the school play I agreed. She later explained that if students could see me (Mr. Cool) doing something like this, others would follow suit. We also prepared for and entered the one act play competition at the state level. I had the lead as a demented old man "Mud Calf Medford". I got to talk to myself and beat myself down the street with a stick, always hearing voices, mostly of children or women. I was the only male in the cast. Our team won that competition as a school. And the leading lady and I were both awarded State Outstanding Actress and Actor for 1963. I enjoyed drama a lot more than I ever dreamed I would. Never once have I regretted the decision to be involved in drama. My wife and I still enjoy plays and musicals. We have attended the theater in various countries during our travels as well as those in the states. A whole new area of art and entertainment opened to me, all because Mrs. McBride believed that I could make a difference. If I would take the lead, others would follow.

It is the same in our Christian walk through life. We are to set the example. That others may follow.

John 13:35 NLT "Your love for one another will prove to the world that you are my disciples".

I had a chance and a reason to call Lynn and Jane some years ago and I took that as an opportunity to let them know that as teachers they made a difference in my life. The role model they demonstrated and the interest they took in their students was noticed and not wasted at least not on me. I also found that, like myself, they believe in Christ. At some point in their lives they became aware of the very same thing I have stated repeatedly. "There are some things in life that only God can get you through". I wonder how many people in our lives we encounter that make a difference as they did, people that we never think to thank. And we never think to ask the question "why me God". What did I do to be singled out? To have these people involved in my life. Whatever it was "Thank You". The rest of my junior year at Imperial was really nothing very exciting. Colorado was only a few miles away and the drinking age was 18. Any 16 year old with half a brain could fake an ID and buy beer in Colorado so we did. We drank a lot; our excuse being what else is there to do in South West Nebraska. I didn't have my own car but it was always easy getting a bunch of guys together and head for Holyoke, Colorado. I did go out for track that spring but I wasn't at all dedicated to the sport. I could pole vault about 12'6" and long jump about 20'6" and I ran the 400 in 56 seconds nothing really all that great. I was just there to be part of the team and stay in somewhat reasonable shape for football.

I wish I could say that I started my senior football season with the same flair as I did my first game the previous year but that wasn't the case. We played as best we could and we won probably 6 or 7 games while losing 3 or 4. The coach still called me Chicago and did several things that my previous coaches would never have thought to say or do.

Basketball was a different story. If I remember correctly we had a record of 25 and 2. It was predicted we would go to the state tournament but our last loss was district finals and only the 1st place team from each district went to the State Tournament. We played a lousy game and lost to a team we should have beaten easily but it was their day to shine not ours.

By the time I started playing basketball at Imperial my junior year I had become fairly proficient at passing and dribbling behind my back. I practiced with the left hand as well as my right. I stayed in the gym as long as I could. Each day dribbling between chairs and passing to an imaginary spot on the wall. At first the coach wasn't in favor of me doing that in games. None the less we eventually agreed that if I lost the ball because of my behind the back antics he would bench me. I'm sure I probably lost the ball a few times but I was accurate more often than I wasn't. I don't know that he ever pulled me out because of a lost ball or a bad pass.

During that 1963-1964 season of my senior year I received two awards. The first was from the Omaha Newspaper. Each week they selected one kid in the state to be the Star of the week. I received a card and a small write up in the Omaha paper as to why I had been selected that particular week I didn't pay much attention to the award at the time but looking back I believe that it was quite a compliment to be that one student athlete singled out in the entire state.

The second award came at the end of basketball season when I was selected to the All-State Team. I was in school and everyone was congratulating me. However, I had no Idea why. The coach finally saw me and explained that in Nebraska they pick 12 players to comprise the All-State team. The same number of players that are on a team. There are five that are considered the team and the other seven are on the team but are not part of the elite five. I was one of the seven. But still if what the coach said was accurate I was considered by the sports writers and coaches to be one of the best high school basketball players in Nebraska that year. That's not a bad way to end your high school athletic career.

I didn't go out for track that year I decided I needed to work as much as possible and I no longer felt the need to train for any sport. Sometime before I graduated the coach had told me of five different colleges that were interested or had made offers that I could consider, but I wasn't interested. In fact I talked to one coach who told me about his program. I still had an attitude. I really wasn't trying to be a smart aleck; although, my response certainly wouldn't support that. I told him I didn't think there was much he could teach me. He agreed, and the conversation was over.

Since I didn't have to train for anything I reverted back to my previous lifestyle, I drank a lot and ran around a lot. I rarely did homework and usually had someone let me use theirs or help me do it. Two of Mom's favorite things to tell me were that unless I graduated from high school I wouldn't amount to anything. I would end up being a plumber or a garbage collector. I personally think both are great career choices. The other thing she frequently said was that I would never live to see my 21st birthday. She had been telling me that since I was 12 when I first started drinking, becoming a problem and getting out of control. However, I did graduate. And to the best of my knowledge I was the first Salsbury to ever receive a high school diploma. I tease my wife about this because we graduated in the same standing in our respective classes She was 26th in her graduating class and so was I. She probably had about 700 in her class and I had 33 in mine.

WHY PLAY BALL

Perhaps this is a good a place as any to describe why I played ball and what it has meant to me over the years. Some kids play with a goal of college, then professional ball and all of the glory and wealth that comes with that. I played because I loved to play and it made me feel equal to all of the other kids. I knew I would never be big enough or have the skill set required to play professionally. But it was the one place I could prove I was as good as anyone else. Not just as an athlete but as a person, and as an individual. I know now that I could have accomplished the same thing scholastically, but I didn't. God gave me the talent to be an athlete and I was able to develop that talent. He didn't reveal that I could have excelled scholastically until much later in my life. One other critical decision point was that athletics is fun and rewarding. Scholastics to me was only rewarding. It required a lot of hard work and was not much fun. When I played ball even practice was fun. I have found very few people in my life that felt studying for the big exam was anyway near as much fun as practicing for the big game. As I had done in most things I chose the easy way; sports.

Coming from the background that I had, I always felt inferior to those kids who had parents and were from what I considered to be a normal life. As an athlete when I walked out on the field or the floor. I was as good as any of them. I never thought about where I came from or that I had less material things than other children my age. What I'm trying to convey is that until the final whistle blew I possessed something that most students didn't have. It was my time to be special. As a person I was as good as anyone for those few minutes, or at least that is how I felt. I know now that those feelings of resentment weren't necessary. God made each one of us uniquely different and special and I was one of the uniquely different individuals. God doesn't make mistakes and regardless of my circumstances and regardless of what I had been told growing up "I was not a mistake." It took years for me to understand this simple concept of a loving father.

As an athlete I was also able to cross all of the normal social, economic and educational boundaries. Those boundaries that all students know exist between the various classes of students. I could hang out with the jocks because athletically I was their equal. I could hang out with the smart kids even though my grades were terrible. Most high school kids like their school athletes and will overlook the grades, and besides my brain worked as well as theirs I just didn't use it. I could also cross the line to be with the hoods and trouble makers without question because I was one of them. I was one who was doing something out of the ordinary and their acceptance was without question. This group had no ulterior motives. To me they were real and I was one of them.

GRADUATION

Graduation night for me was uneventful except for a few cans of spray paint that was used around the county to proclaim that the Senior Class of 1964 had arrived. There were three of us involved. As I was writing this it occurred to me, that had I done this during football or basketball season the principal probably would not have even considered me as one of the culprits. But since this was spring and I wasn't doing track I was just another student that was suspect because of who he was, where he came from, and mostly who he ran around with. I understand now that your choice of friends make an impact on what others see in you. I don't believe that who you hang out with defines who you are because Christ hung out with sinners. However, it certainly puts a bias on what other see in you. This was something that totally escaped me as I was growing up. Even though I had been told several times to find new friends. For this particular act of vandalism I was the first person the principle called to the office. I had paint on my hands and on my shoes. However, for a good reason I denied any knowledge of the event at that time. One member of our trio had a pretty extensive record of violations including a felony. I knew that if we involved him, the other two of us would fall hard just so he could be taken in. I wanted to talk to the other two and relay my plan. We all agreed, the two of us turned ourselves in to the local policeman as the culprits. Protecting the one with a felony record and ourselves as well.

When all was said and done it was determined that we would repaint all of the articles we had painted. A house, a bunch of signs, guard rails, a gasoline transport truck and a grain elevator or two. This amounted to about $5000.00 in damages. We also had to face the student body and tell them of our vandalism. I told them to use water based paint next year. I got a pretty big laugh from the student body but not from the principal. I and one other person spent a lot of Saturdays, Sundays and after work during the summer restoring the damage we did in a few hours one evening because of a poor choice. With every choice there is a consequence that is not always good or not always bad but irreversible none the less. My involvement in this incident would be questioned in less than two years when I least expected or wanted it to reappear and by an individual that definitely had my attention.

After graduation I stayed with Jim and Suzie most of the time. I worked at the hardware store, drank every weekend and for the most part ran around making a fool of myself. I managed to save enough money to buy a 1957 Chevy for $595.00. While other kids were getting ready for college and a few guys going in the service. I decided to just stay in Imperial and work at the store until I was 21. It had been suggested that I would possibly get my own store to manage when I was somewhere close to that age. The idea of staying in Imperial was great during the summer when everyone was still in town. However, when everyone left in the fall and the kids younger than I had all gone back to high school it was different. I was no longer the local athlete that everyone looked up to. I wasn't on the field on Friday night. Someone else had taken my place and I couldn't handle it. I went to games on Friday nights and watched a struggling team on the field. I was critical of the quarterback, the coach, and the plays they ran. Everything was wrong. I followed the team through part of the season going to all of the home games and away games as well. At the games I would get the comments from the fans and students of "wish you were still playing" or "we sure miss you on the field" but while the sentiment was nice it just wasn't the same. I wanted to be out there but I had missed my chance of playing in college. Knowing that it was no one's fault but my own didn't make it any easier. I had turned down college and I was regretting that decision.

THE NIGHT THAT CHANGED IT ALL...

It wasn't unusual for me to drink and even get drunk after a Friday night game. I can't say why I decided this particular night to start drinking earlier than usual but I did. On this night I started long before the opening kickoff. I started before I even got to the town where the game was to be played. Imperial was playing a town in Colorado so a few friends and I stopped at a bar in Holyoke Colorado on the way to the game. Things got out of control. By the time we showed up at the game I had already been kicked out of the bar in Holyoke. A bar that I had been frequenting since I was 16. A place in which I was well known thanks to a fake ID and lack of scrutiny on the part of the owners. By the time I showed up at the game, I had no business being there. I can't tell you all of the things that transpired that night and maybe it's just as well. It's too bad; sad actually that anyone drinks to the extent that they are no longer in control of themselves. I had previously been pretty drunk many times in my life. Like the night I drove my 57 Chevy in the lake because I thought the area to my left was so smooth the road must be over there. That's right I drove that car far enough into the lake that when I opened the door water came pouring in. I had visions of fish swimming around in my car. But even then I was in better control of myself than I was this particular night.

What I'm about to say is only my opinion. I'm not a Doctor and I may be wrong. However, since I'm writing I get to share some of what I believe to be true. That being said; I believe that if I were an alcoholic I would have a disease. A disease that some say is not controllable by the person until they get help. I've even been told it is no different than any other disease in that it is not their fault they have it. But it is their fault if they don't seek help to control their use of alcohol. Therefore, I split those who drink excessively into two categories.

There are alcoholics and there are drunks. In my opinion these are two distinct, separate individuals each with a different problem. An alcoholic hasn't any control of their drinking and gets drunk because he or she possess a disease something they need help to overcome. On the contrary a drunk doesn't necessarily have a disease but chooses of their own free will to put themselves and others in danger because of their selfishness. They may think about the danger and damage to others but they just don't care. I was a drunk. Plain and simple. I chose to go out and get drunk, drive fast and not have control of my body or my reflexes. This choice endangered others as well as myself. I predetermined I was going to do exactly that each time before I stepped out the door, Having said, that I have no sympathy for a drunk, but I do have some understanding of those who are alcoholics. I'm not proud of myself or many of the things I did during this time in my life. At the time I was lying to myself pretending to have fun and to continue to enjoy the popularity I experienced as an athlete the year before. This was a very shallow existence. Fame only lasts until the next season or the next star comes along. I went back to my high school once after 20 years. All of the trophies and plaques with my name on them had been replaced by someone bigger, better and faster than I was.

It would be great if I could say that I gave up alcohol completely after that night but that wasn't the case. Most of the time if I were going out, I would go to a different town than the one I lived in. I still drank in excess for a long time after that night because I was immature, and selfish. I hadn't exactly had anyone in my life helping me to mature or teaching me to make the wise decisions. Decisions that would be considerate of the other people. I made no effort to realize or even care that others may accidentally be affected by what I was doing. However, that doesn't excuse the fact that it was me making those poor choices. I was 18 and had been making my own decisions since I started drinking at age 12. Ultimately, I was responsible for whatever I did and I knew that.

The morning after this particular Friday night's game I woke up in the back seat of my car in a strange garage. I had no idea whose garage I was in, or how I had gotten there, but I knew I didn't feel all that well. I managed to get the door of my car and the garage door open and I stumbled out into the day. I knocked on the door of the house that seemed associated with the garage and found I was in the garage of my friend. The one who was the third part of the trio that had painted the town graduation night. The one with the record. The one that I chose to protect. Apparently he had driven my car home parked it in the garage and just left me there in the back seat. He told me a few of the things I had done that night laughing all the while. He told me how I had yelled at a few people during last night's game staggering in front of people in the stands. The same people that only last year thought I was something out of the ordinary. And now by my own choice I was just another 18 year old drunk from Imperial Nebraska.

I had to go to work that day and I was not looking forward to a confrontation with Jim. My only hope was that he had not seen what I had done. However, he had seen me, and he informed me that his biggest concern was that as we were going home he was doing 80 and I passed him like he was barely moving. He said I must have been doing 100. His only comment of reprimand was that younger kids still looked up to me and I needed to be aware of that. To a lot of the boys in grade school who wanted to play ball I was still their hero. I think those few words hurt more than if he had fired me. I didn't have the heart to tell him I was in the back seat passed out and it wasn't me driving. What had happened? How could I have made such a fool of myself in front of the people who had trusted me and put their faith in me as a person and as an athlete? How many others had I offended that night? I will never know. I'm sure there were many. I wondered if I would end up like some of the men in town that all the kids made fun of, the ones who staggered home on Friday and Saturday nights? Would I turn out just like my Grandmother said dead before my 21st birthday? Maybe the principal in Naches was correct I shouldn't be around decent people. I didn't have any answers, but I knew something had to change.

YOU'RE PRETTY SMART

I talked to Jim later that week and told him I had decided to leave Imperial, to leave the hardware store, and the career they had planned for me. I was leaving to join the Navy. My brother Clancy had joined when he was only 17 and Jim had done the same thing when he was young. So the Navy seemed like a good place to go. Besides I knew that it was only a matter of time before I would be drafted into the Army if I didn't do something. The various recruiters came into town from McCook (a larger town) about once a month or so. The Navy recruiter was there this week and I went to talk with him. This recruiter influenced my life but he has no idea to what extent. I was informed that I had to take some tests before I could enlist to determine what I was going to be qualified to do in the Navy. I took the exam and he came back with my results and made this statement, "wow, I've never had someone score this well on the exam before". "You can do anything in the Navy you want." "Go to any school the Navy has to offer enlisted men." I certainly didn't feel all that smart, and I had no idea how I scored that high on the tests but I did. It was late October and almost getting to be winter weather. He was wearing his Dress Blue Uniform with all of his medals and ribbons and whatever else he was able or required to place on his sleeve and chest. I did the only practical thing any 18 year old would have done. I took a look at his uniform and said I wanted to wear all that stuff pointing to his rate, his dolphins and his patrol pin. "I want to wear that," I stated. He explained that he was a nuclear electrician and that to attend the schools and training required I would have to enlist for 6 years. Even I can do the math I'll only be 24 when I get out. I can handle it. And so I did; I enlisted for 6 years so I could go to Nuclear Power School and wear dolphins and a patrol pin, be an electrician, look impressive and get out of Imperial.

I left for boot camp in San Diego on November 17th 1964. No goodbyes, no crying sweetheart, just me getting on the bus. I said goodbye to Jim, Suzie and the kids at the house before I left. The Navy had promised that I would be able to attend Electricians Mate "A" school after boot camp and then Nuclear Training after that. The only caveat was that the Navy would see that I was given the opportunity to attend the schools. However, if I were to flunk out or fail any part of my training, I still owed Uncle Sam 6 years of my life. It would be considered my fault if I couldn't handle the training. Boot Camp was a breeze for me. Due to a couple of events during boot camp it was noticed that I was in better shape than most of the recruits and I was assigned the task of Athletic Petty Officer. My job was to get our company; Company 636, ready for the athletic events that each company participated in prior to graduation from boot camp. I also had to make certain that everyone in our company could swim. No one was to be left behind because they couldn't pass the required swimming test. On more than one occasion I wanted to teach them the same way I was taught. Just throw them in the pool and let them sink or swim. With this assignment came certain benefits as well. For instance I didn't have to do KP duty (kitchen duty) with the rest of my company. When they were getting up at 0400 to do menial work in the mess hall. I was getting up at 0600 to go to the gym or the pool to teach non swimmers how to pass the swimming requirement to be in the Navy. Not a bad assignment. I often wondered why anyone would join the Navy if they couldn't swim.

I certainly wasn't prone to being homesick like some recruits. Some of these guys just wanted out and to go home to something familiar; a girl, a mother and not so much physical and mental abuse. I heard rumor of a guy in the next barracks from ours who hated it so much he felt death was a better option. He jumped out of a window with a rope around his neck but he had too much rope and when he hit the ground he broke both legs. He got out of the Navy but he didn't have to die. There were some in my company that left in the night thinking they could get a ride from someone. Somehow they wanted to get back to whatever state they had come from. I, on the other hand was thriving, three meals a day, sleep on a regular basis, a routine or regimen was exactly what I needed. I loved it.

When Boot Camp ended 12 weeks later about Feb 1965. I went back to Imperial to visit Jim and Suzie and to say hi to Mom and Gene. I found out that during that 12 week absence, Mom had sold all of the guns I had acquired (I assume for alcohol) and she had put my 57 Chevy on its side in a ditch. I assume alcohol was involved in that also. Jim and Suzie let me use their car while I was there if I needed to go anywhere even though the Chevy was drivable it just looked bad all scraped and dented down the side. I had two weeks and I spent it with Jim, Suzie and the kids.

I saw Mom one more time before she died in 1971. She and Gene had moved to Colorado Springs; I was driving through there in the summer of 1967 with a friend on our way to the east coast for some additional training. We stopped and talked with them for a few hours long enough to find out that she had wrecked the 57 Chevy again; this time totaling it. I never saw Mom again but I did attend her funeral in 1971. It would be 20 years before I returned to visited Imperial again. When I left Imperial after my boot camp visit I was headed back to San Diego for Electricians Mate School. I wasn't a great student in that school but I did ok. I also found Tijuana, Mexico on the weekends. Not a good match for someone like me. I'm not going to say a lot about my visits there, other than I went there and I went there as often as I could and did crazy stupid things. I had a friend that was Hispanic. He and I were well known by the owners, workers and bouncers of several places due to some of the antics we pulled during our visits. I have a tattoo on my arm that probably explains it best. It is a Skull and Cross Bones. I was known by some people as "Doc"; that's what is engraved under the Skull on my arm. That tattoo cost me $8.00 and fortunately that is all the money I had or I would have finished my original intentions for that arm. My Hispanic friend and several others we ran around with referred to me as "Doc el Diablos Companero". (Doc the devils Companion). The American version of a Hispanic phrase. I am so thankful that I didn't have the extra $8.00 that night to add those words to my arm. My wife claims that if I had a tattoo on my arm that said The Devils Companion, she would not have married me. Today I look at the word "DOC" It reminds me of what I was and not what I am. I prefer to change the acronym to mean "Disciple of Christ" that is what I want to be and I work at that every day of my life. It is a far better goal than what I was trying to be at that point in my life. It wasn't that I was so mean or that I was delving into the dark side of Tijuana. It was simply the look I mentioned earlier. That look that made a statement; a statement that this person really doesn't care about anything, that he has no feelings. Therefore it's probably best to just leave him alone. That is why they gave me that name. But, it's not who I am

Being in the Navy Nuclear Program in the 1960 s required a fairly high security clearance and it was explained to me that it didn't take much to lose that clearance. I needed to stay out of trouble for the next 5-1/2 years that was left on my enlistment. Otherwise, I could be removed from the program as a security risk. More than a couple of speeding tickets was just cause for loss of a clearance and a DUI was a given that your clearance would probably be pulled. At least that was the threat given to me. I realized that if I wanted to wear all the stuff my recruiter did and serve on a submarine, I needed to clean it up.

I arrived at Mare Island Naval Base in California about Mid-January or early February of 1966 scheduled to attend a school for what was predicted to be the hardest scholastic endeavor that most of us had ever faced. In six months we were going to study **Math, Physics, Nuclear physics, Thermodynamics, (heat transfer and fluid flow characteristics) Chemistry, Electronics, Electricity and Mechanics.** I think this was about the time I got a wake-up call. Look at those subjects and think about this, the only subject on that entire list that I had even the remotest idea of what it was, is math. I had taken freshman algebra and the coach was my teacher. I passed with a D. We were about to begin a math class that would start with basic math end with integral calculus in six months. Only a few would be lucky or skilled enough to graduate.

I suppose it took about two weeks for our class officer a Lieutenant who was also our Physics instructor, to get to Salsbury (alphabetically) as he performed his review and evaluations of each class member. I was called to his office and his first words were something to the effect of "So you think you are Rembrandt". I had no idea whatsoever what he was talking about. I didn't know who Rembrandt was. I'm sure I must have just sat there with this deer in the headlight look. He explained it this way. You must like to paint? Then it hit me that during my background check for my security clearance the painting on graduation night must have come up. We discussed the matter for a bit but he assured me it wouldn't have an impact on my clearance. "Whew" that was a relief. However, the next words out of his mouth went something like this.

"You won't need a security clearance. I'm looking at your transcripts and I'd like to know how on earth you ever managed to get here. You took nothing in high school to prepare you for this school, and I can assure you that nobody in this Navy gives a rip about how far you can throw a football. Almost all of the students here have had some college or at least college prep classes. You took absolutely nothing". You have no business being in this school. I really got the impression that he was more than just a little mad about something. I have no idea if what he told me is absolutely true but this is what he said next. "Salsbury only 1% of all the sailors who enlist score high enough to get into the Navy's nuclear program. Of that 1% only 10% actually sign up for it. And of that 10% half of them flunk out before they ever leave this school. I don't know what your recruiter told you but I'm telling you that you will be the first to leave and that you will be gone in two weeks. In the meantime go back to class and stay out of trouble."

I did as I was told but in two weeks I was still in school. In two months I was still there. And when we graduated at the end of six months. I was still there. My schedule during that six months was mostly self-imposed and was something like this. Classes started at 0800 and ran until 1600 with a 1 hr. lunch break. At 1600 most students were free for the rest of the night. I went to dinner until 1800 then I was back in the common study area locked in a booth about the size of a phone booth and I studied until 2200. Then off to my room where I had a friend who tutored me in math and Chemistry my two least favorite subjects. At the end of the training I graduated with a GPA of 2.57 the Navy required a 2.50 to graduate. The commanding officer called me into his office just before finals and informed me that he had been personally watching my progress over the last 6 months and with only a final oral exam left he was positive I was not going to fail.

He was administering my oral exam himself. Consider for a moment the odds of me being able to get through Nuclear Power School. I never took a hard class the entire time I was in school. In fact my senior year I had 3 study halls and helped coach the freshman team during my last class of the day. If not for that I would have had 4 study halls. And yet I managed to make it through this incredibly difficult Navy school. To me this is on the same plane as walking away from that accident when I was a freshman in high school. Or throwing three touchdown passes in less than two minutes to make my debut into a new town and a fresh start in Nebraska. There are times and circumstances in our lives that God definitely helps us through. This had to be one of them. This opened the path that would be my career as I matured and eventually left the Navy.

The next step was a year of training in the desert of Idaho (prototype). A weird place for a sailor (no water). We lived in houses in Idaho Falls, and trained in the desert at the Idaho National Experimental Lab (INEL) and had a fifty four mile bus ride each way every day. I did this school a little differently, I didn't ride the bus that often. Somehow I managed to anger a 1ˢᵗ Class Petty Officer (E-6) that was shorter than I was. He had no sense of humor when I put my arm on his shoulder and ask how my little buddy was today. I spent the next 11 weeks restricted to the site. I was allowed to go to town on Saturday afternoon to do laundry and buy food. The strange thing about this, was that he intended to punish me. He wanted me out of the program but it didn't turn out that way. I had more time to study and train. Therefore, it was actually a blessing so I chose to continue that schedule for almost all of the remainder of my time at prototype. I am reminded of the scripture in Genesis where Joseph tells his brothers that (paraphrased) **"what man intends for harm God intends for good"**. This was true in this case as well as in the instance where my principal at Naches High School gave me the choice of jail or Nebraska. In both cases it was the best thing that could have happened in my life. However, I did manage to take a few of my off days and explore the hills of Idaho and Yellowstone Park and of course engaging in an occasional party with the local people my age.

This part of our training was the hands on approach. Here we actually learned about all of the mechanics that the previous six months of classroom training had been preparing us for. We used wrenches and operated turbines, generators and of course, the reactor. We could trace the steam lines, hydraulic lines, air lines and all of the other sub components involved in operating a reactor to produce steam and power. I excelled at this; it was easy for me. But for some, especially those with little mechanical aptitude, it was rough. It was as hard for some of them as it was for me during that 1st six months of classroom training. I became the tutor for those who had been helping me. I graduated 2nd in my class going from the bottom to the top. As I look back at that training I am amazed, totally in awe of what God can do. I was an E-3 when I arrived in Idaho and was promoted to E-4 before I left. I was also asked if I would like to stay on and be an instructor, what a switch that would have been. However, it wasn't in my plan to stay. I wanted a submarine in the ocean, and Dolphins on my chest, and a Patrol Pin with stars and all the other things my recruiter wore that were so impressive that day. And nothing was going to stop me.

TAKE A RIDE

On August 7th of 1967 I received my orders and reported to the USS Daniel Webster SSBN 626 in Charleston SC

The Webster was a Fleet Ballistic Missile Submarine referred to as a boomer. We carried 16 nuclear missiles and was propelled by a reactor similar to the one I had just trained on in Idaho.

I went to sea on a submarine for the first time on August 10th 1967 my 21st birthday. I can't describe the mixed feelings I had. On one hand I was scared out of my mind even though my training had taught me how safe a submarine actually was. At the same time I was excited beyond belief that I was actually going to be able to go beneath the surface of the ocean to depths I could only imagine. It was hard to control my anxiety. That day was a day I will never forget. We were only going out to sea for 3 days on a sea trial. This was intended to test everything and make sure it all worked prior to leaving on a 2 ½ month patrol about a week later. On August 11th we were still under water and I breathed a sigh of relief. Mom was wrong. I did live to see my 21st birthday and I'm not a plumber or a garbage collector (still in my opinion two very good trades). However, I was a nuclear electrician and someday I would look as impressive as my recruiter.

When we left Charleston to go on patrol we submerged and did not surface until it was time to return to Charleston some 70 odd days later.

Mid way through my 2nd patrol I qualified to wear those dolphins I had wanted so much. And I had a patrol pin with a star for each patrol we went out on. I truly was starting to look just like that recruiter.

The Navy told me that if I would re-enlist for one extra year I could get a bonus and extra pay. That sounded great so I did. I took some of my money and made a down payment on a 1968 Firebird and took off for Christmas vacation to visit Jim and Suzie who had moved to South Dakota. It was there that they had their eighth child. Jim and Suzie were excited that I was going to be there for Christmas and Jim wanted me to meet the student nurse who was with him and Suzie during the delivery of #8. She had become a family friend just as I had during my high school years in Imperial.

I really wasn't all that excited about meeting some girl from a college I had never heard of. However, as I stated before, Jim could sell refrigerators in Antarctica. So I agreed.

I met Carol Ann Lund on January 3rd 1968 in the hallway of Augustana College in Sioux Falls, South Dakota. Jim went into her class room interrupted the class and brought her out to the hallway just to meet me. Neither of us were all that impressed at the time and both of us were very embarrassed. However, just to appease Jim we both agreed to go out for dinner that evening. We went out the next two nights as well. I left to go back to Charleston 3 days after I had met Carol. I was returning to Charleston S.C. to do another 70 to 75 days underwater. Carol and I could not contact each other during this time. There were no messages or love letters sent to the boat in those days. And I had none waiting for me when I returned to the surface. But when I did return to the surface I headed for South Dakota and ask her to marry me. She said yes. We were together for 10 days just long enough to buy a ring and meet her parents in St. Paul, Minnesota. I went back to Charleston and then to Newport News, Virginia. There Carol joined me and we were married on July 5th 1968 after only 3 actual dates and a total of only 13 days together. The uniform that I wanted to wear to make me look just like my recruiter, the one that I thought would be so impressive was never seen by Carol until after we were married. There are times when God has a much better idea of what you need than you can ever comprehend. This was one of those times. In Jerimiah 29: 11 (NIV) God say's "For I know the plans I have for you, plans to prosper you and not to harm you, plans to give you hope and a future".

He was true to his word I had a future and I wouldn't be a plumber or garbage collector as Mom had predicted (Still two very good career choices).

Before we were married I made two promises to Carol, and I have kept both of them. Two things that were important to her for personal reasons. She didn't ask me to make the 1st one but I understood that is was something she wanted and why that it would be important to her. For that reason it was important to me as well.

First: No longer would I drink in excess or stop at bars after work.

Second: If she were to ever get pregnant I would quit smoking completely.

We had our first child almost two years after we were married and I quit smoking the day she told me that I was to be a father. From 3 packs a day to nothing and I have never regretted it. That was in 1969 and Brad our 1st son was born in 1970 in a smoke free environment. I doubt seriously that I would still be alive today if I had consumed 3 packs a day since 1969. God's plan is always for our good. Amazing isn't it??

For family reasons Carol and I decided to leave the Navy when my 7 years were up. I loved the Navy life, but, it was not what I wanted for us and I loved her and our son more than the Navy. I didn't like the 2 ½ to 3 month separation from her and our son every time I went on patrol. Our first child Brad was born in Hawaii at the Army hospital. I was In Guam at the time preparing for another patrol when I was told that there were complications with the pregnancy and the skipper was sending me home to be there for the delivery of my child. Everyone knew that the baby was to be induced except Carol. I showed up unannounced on April 18th and drove her straight to the hospital. Brad was born on April 19th. Everything went great with no complications, with either the Mom or the baby. Carol and Brad went home with me on the morning of April 20th and I left that same day to return to Guam and another 70 plus days of patrol.

In December of 1971 my ride was over I had accomplished what I wanted when I joined the Navy. I was a Nuclear Electrician, I was an EM 1(SS) with Dolphins and a Patrol Pin with Stars just like my recruiter. However, none of that mattered any longer.

Carol and I had many great times with the friends we made on the boat, and the places we went. The sailors and families on a submarine are a different bunch. It's hard explain how close we were. Even though it has been almost 50 years since I left the Navy we still have friends that we see and keep in contact with.

THEY WERE CORRECT

The infamous **everyone or they** that we have all heard about was absolutely correct. They told me that with the Navy training I had received getting a job as a civilian would not be an issue.

I was discharged on December 1st 1971 and went to work for Northern states Power Company in Minnesota close to where Carol had grown and attended school. Of course she still had family there and Jim and Suzie still lived in Sioux Falls, South Dakota well within driving distance for an occasional visit.

James (Jamie) our second child was born 4 months after I got out of the Navy and since Carol was pregnant before I started working it was considered a pre-existing condition therefore, no insurance. The doctor asked about insurance and we told him we would just pay until our bill was paid in full. No need, he said the hospital would only charge us for the days that she was actually in the hospital. And his service would be minimal. We brought Jamie home just a couple of days after he was born and settled into a normal life for two young parents.

I'm not going to go through the career path that I choose at this time, but I will say that all during my working career I was blessed. We managed to make enough to be able to live on a single income (something we both wanted) this allowed Carol to be able to stay at home and be a Mom. (Definitely a full time job).

I was also fortunate to be able to work in many different positions and with several companies. Moving each time for a promotion. I took a few college classes that interested me, and a few that I felt would help me excel in my career. I primarily relied on my Navy training and it served me well.

From 1993 until I retired in 2016 (at least I think I'm retiring) I worked for the government managing projects with budgets at times reaching in excess of $ 50 million dollars annually. Supervising people far more educated than I was. All those years of being an athlete had taught me to be a leader and I was successful in motivating people to accomplish whatever task we were assigned. I can truthfully say that looking back at my career, God has been very generous. I may not be a CEO or president of a company but I am a man who came from the humble beginnings of working as a migrant fruit picker to become the manager of skilled people. The work, the people, and the projects that I have been responsible for has been quite a transition. I thank God every day for giving me those opportunities and putting people in my life that believed in me.

Had that Lieutenant been correct and had I flunked out of Nuclear Power School my entire life would have been different. To everyone but God it was obvious that I didn't belong there. However, I am sure He had other things in mind for my life

LET'S EXPAND

After Carol and I left the Navy and moved to the Minnesota area we settled in a small town on the Wisconsin, Minnesota border. I was commuting to Bayport Minnesota each day to work in the power plant that had given me a job.

We had purchased our first home and were doing quite well attending the Lutheran church in town and making friends, and of course, I was playing ball.

Carol had noticed an article in one of the local papers regarding the fate of the Amer-Asian orphans from Viet Nam. The article explained in detail the need for families to adopt. Like we did most things and not unlike when we got married, the suggestion was made to adopt and our answer was yes. We were on our way to adopt our first child, Kim, a girl from Viet Nam only 7 months old.

Kim's story and the circumstances of her adoption are another story of the Grace of God in our family. The fact that she is alive today is not only a testimony of her will to survive but also of God's Grace to us and to her.

Carol and I had spent months filling out paper work completing home studies and sending money to Viet Nam for the paper work required to adopt in that country. The volumes of paper that never seemed to end can be overwhelming. On one of the home visits the social worker gave Carol and I a lists of questions to answer. One of those questions was stated as such "when did you meet your spouse" Carol answered the question honestly explaining about college and Jim and Suzie and all the other things surrounding our very short courtship. I, on the other hand looked at the question and answered directly and to the point, "January 3, 1968". This was not exactly what she was after, but it is was what was asked. I suppose it was about a year after we started the adoption process that we were informed that our daughter Kim was going to arrive at the Minneapolis airport. We were aware that her health was in question and that she would need to see a doctor after her arrival. The day came and we were so excited waiting for all of the other children to depart the plane and watching other families as they saw their child for the first time. Our daughter Kim came to us in the arms of a friend wrapped in a blanket. We carefully pulled it back to see our precious little child, thinking she was sleeping and not wanting to disturb her. We were shocked.

She was malnourished, her head had been shaved to accommodate the IVs required to keep her alive in Viet Nam and on the plane ride to the US. What hair she had stuck straight up and seemed stiff or bristly. Her skin hung on the tiny frame and appeared to have nothing under it but bones. The decision was made instantly we were going straight to the hospital from the airport. Someone suggested Children's Hospital St. Paul. We left the airport knowing we were headed to Children's but having no idea exactly where it was. It seemed as though my car had a mind of its own and I drove directly to the hospital I had never seen. Not once did we miss a road or turn to get there. Arriving at the hospital we were met at the emergency room entrance and asked if this was the child with the high fever. I hadn't the slightest idea who that child may have been but I answered yes she has a fever

Our child was taken from us by a medical team of pediatric doctors and nurses. Sometime later that night an intern informed us that it was doubtful Kim would make it through the night. Kim was 7 months old and weighed a mere 7 pounds. We were told to go home and comeback tomorrow. We were devastated, disappointed and confused. Even though we hadn't bonded physically with Kim we had bonded in our minds we had seen pictures, had been around other families who had adopted. We wanted to take our child home. Instead an intern was telling us to go home and that there was very little possibility that she would survive the night.

We came back the next day and were told that she was a fighter and that she had a chance to survive. But she would require hospitalization for quite some time to receive the medication required to keep her alive.

As the weeks went by Carol spent almost every day in the hospital holding Kim every moment she was allowed, bonding with her and learning to care for her. With all of the medical conditions Kim had upon arrival to the U.S. this was no easy task.

Five weeks after that first night time ride from the airport we made another trip to Children's Hospital, this time as a family to bring our baby home. She was very small. She required special formula since she had a milk intolerance and she was so small she seemed fragile. But she was doing great. And what a set of lungs she had.

The war in Viet Nam was coming to an end and the need for adoptive parents was becoming more critical each day. Carol and I decided to adopt our 2nd child from Viet Nam. This time a two year old girl we named Cherie. Cherie at two years old was potty-trained, brushed her teeth on her own, ate solid food, had pierced ears and was probably one of the healthiest and the most organized two year old to leave Viet Nam. I mention this only because to me it certainly points to the fact that she was obviously cared for and loved before she had to be lifted from Viet Nam. We have no idea why she was placed in the orphanage but my assumption is that her parents were either deceased or felt it was the only way to save their daughter's life. She came to the U.S. on one of the last planes leaving Viet Nam before the country collapsed and adoptions were no longer an option for the children who were left behind.

Shortly after Cherie's adoption we moved to Bayport, Minnesota a sleepy little town on the St. Croix River. Carol and I had always known we wanted a large family. Therefore, we decided the time was right to adopt again. We could have had more biological children, however, our feeling was why. When there were so many children in foster care waiting to be adopted. We went to the State Office and applied for a child from the State of Minnesota, when and if one were to become available. We were prepared for the fact that it may take a while to adopt an American child regardless of color. However, we had done our homework and we didn't really care about the ethnicity of the child. The social worker informed us that regardless of race the wait would be long and that our odds of getting a blonde haired blue eyed child was almost an impossibility. After all, we already have 4 children. She predicted that if we were to put our name on the waiting list today, it would take approximately 7 years before we would be eligible for the adoption of another child.

Our response was easy, "great put us on the list; that's about what we were planning for anyway." We figured by then all of our children would be in school and somewhat independent. There ages at this time were 8, 6, 5, and 4. In 7 years they would be the perfect ages for a younger sibling to enter our house.

We were happy with that scenario so we returned to our house on Third Avenue in Bayport, Minnesota. Having 7 years to plan for our next child.

Surprise, the seven years had miraculously became just a few weeks. The social worker called and explained that she had a child in Farmington, Minnesota. Blonde hair and blue eyes. The social worker felt she would blend well into our family. She explained that every time she had gone to the foster home in the past few weeks for some unknown reason our name seemed to come to mind. Our family was what she believed this new child needed. The social worker went on to explain that this was no ordinary child. Amy (that was her name) was seven months old, she had been given up for adoption by a 17 year old mother who resided with her grandparents. The 19 year old father was no longer part of the scenario and the mother didn't feel she would be able to care for a child in her environment. Both parents had experimented or used drugs at some time in their lives. The social worker felt that Amy's development might be better in a different home.

She asked if we could go to the foster home with her on the coming Friday to meet Amy, and to make an on the spot decision if we wanted to bring her into our home or not. We were not given much time to make a decision of that importance. I mean what happened to 7 years? However, we both agreed to go. The social worker would want to know immediately following our visit if we wanted to adopt Amy. But first she wanted to be honest with us making us aware of the fact that Amy had some medical issues we would have to deal with. She had been diagnosed with epilepsy and had, had a grand mall seizure in the Doctor's office while the social worker was present. She had been through all of the brain wave scans and whatever medical test was customary to have at that time. She was on several medications to try and help control her seizures. However, the medications were not working as well as the doctors had hoped. She also was a very irritable child. Amy cried often and was hard to control.

Carol and I knew nothing of epilepsy. We tried to learn as much as possible in a very short time. Our doctor and I spoke on the phone and he explained what we were going to be subjecting ourselves and our children to if we decided to go forward with this adoption. He felt that if we hadn't already had 4 children we would have easily been able to dedicate the time required to handle an epileptic child. However with 4 children already in our house he suggested we proceed with caution knowing what may lay ahead if we continued with our efforts to adopt this child. The more I read the more I was scared that he may be right and that I wouldn't be able to accept her disability. If Carol had similar doubts she didn't share them with me. And so with her calmness and in spite of the warning, and the material we had read we decided to at least go and see this baby. The one thing I did learn that gave me some hope was that childhood epilepsy is sometimes outgrown and may disappear completely by the time a child reaches their late teens or maturity. Also unlike some; this childhood disease is often controllable with medication. But not always.

We weren't allowed to bring our children to the foster home. Our social worker had made arrangements for a co-worker to watch the children while we went for our visit. The social worker had explained to the foster parents that she was bringing a young couple to see the baby and that if we were to decide to adopt her, all of our paper work was in order and we would be removing the child very soon.

Carol and I walked into the foster parent's house and saw a beautiful blond haired, blue eyed baby that came to me, sat in my lap and immediately started playing with the necklace that I had made while on patrol on the submarine in 1967. It was made from a mercury head dime. That same necklace I still wear to this day. Without a word spoken between us, we both knew instantly that Amy would be our child. There was no way we could leave this baby in the foster home for one minute longer than was necessary. We weren't there to pick out a puppy, this was a baby, a real person with a personality and just as lively and alert as any other child I had ever held. We went to our car and the social worker asked what we thought about taking Amy into our family. Of course, we wanted the child. Soon we would have 5 children in our young family. Now we had to actually fill out all of the paper work that we supposedly had previously completed. We went home to wait. But not for long. The social worker called Monday and said let's go pick up your child today. Again the other social worker watched our children while we picked up Amy, her medications and what few clothes she had. When we returned with their new sister, all of the kids were absolutely ecstatic.

But now what? We didn't have a crib, diapers, bottles, or anything. All we had was a baby and a ton of medicine.

The following event happened shortly after we brought Amy home. We were all sitting on the floor with Amy. Carol and I had decided to explain to the children about Amy's condition. Explaining that she would require a lot of our time, and would never be like other normal children. She could have a seizure at any time. We explained what a seizure was and we instructed them that if it happened to just keep her from hurting herself, and to get one of us as fast as possible.

Everyone was sad as well as quiet while we sat there looking at this beautiful girl. When my oldest son Brad simply said "we should pray for her". Carol and I had taken the kids to church and to Sunday school since they were born. But we didn't go to a charismatic church similar to the Pentecostal Church that I had attended as a child. A church that routinely practiced prayer for healing. We attended a Lutheran Church in Minnesota and to pray for healing of a person may have been a little bit of a stretch for that particular congregation.

However, Carol said "that's a great idea, Brad" and so we did. We held hands and we each prayed that God would heal their new little sister.

Carol asked me later that evening "now what are we going to do about Amy's medication"? My answer was as simple as Brad's request to pray. I didn't know at the time exactly what prompted me to say this, but I said it "If you truly believe that God answers prayers take away the medicine." Carol and I had never in our lives done anything like this before nor have we ever done anything remotely like this since. But that night, somehow we knew we were going to do just that. We took away the medicine. Not only did we stop giving Amy any medicine. We went one step further and threw it all out. I'm sure there are some who would question us for doing that, and maybe some that would have attempted to remove Amy from our home had we told others at that time what we had just done.

A few weeks later Carol and Amy went back to the Neurologist for more testing. The Doctor hooked her up to all of the equipment required for the testing and came out to tell Carol that something had happened. Amy's brain waves were as normal as any other child of her age. Today Amy is a wife and mother and has never shown any evidence of epilepsy since that night we all prayed. Feel free to make your own decision as to what happened. I believe it had to be something very similar to my old man in a peach tree or a 7 month old who only weighed 7 pounds and still survived, or even me walking away from a head on collision with an immovable object at 70 MPH.

There are some things that only God can get you through, things you can't explain any other way, and problems, that only he can solve.

1 John 5:14 (NIV)
This is the confidence we have in approaching God: that
if we ask anything according to his will he hears us.

James 1:6 (NIV)
But when you ask. You must believe and not
doubt, because the one who doubts is like a wave
of the sea, blown and tossed by the wind

Mark 11:24 (NIV)
Therefore I tell you, whatever you ask in prayer, believe
that you have received it, and it will be yours.

Our entire family had faith and believed that God would heal Amy.
And he did!

RICKMAN

Several times during our marriage and especially during the time of our adoptions Carol often suggested that I try and find my family. She felt I should find my mother and father and even my younger brother if possible.

I wasn't at all in favor of doing this and I resisted the whole idea for a long time. It was probably very selfish of me. Or maybe it was an act of self-preservation. In either case I just could not imagine this great family reunion with my biological parents. They hadn't wanted me when I was young. Why would I want to see them when they were old? I could understand finding my brother. I thought that would be great, and maybe it would be acceptable to find out who my biological father was. However, since early childhood I had been told by my grandmother that my mother would sleep with anyone that would show her a good time. She didn't accuse her of being one who charges for her services. But she said she was a woman who had little or no morals and as such didn't seem to care who she slept with or the consequences of that action. I heard her refer to Evelyn by those names that were fitting that lifestyle almost as early as I could remember. I knew she had abandoned us in the middle of the night. I was keenly aware that when she dropped us off she never came back. I had been told this story many times in my life. However, I could never understand why she had left us with the very same people that she had ran away from. Why would someone do that? My logical mind says that if it wasn't suitable for her to live that life style, why it would be ok for your children. My opinion was that it would be a decision made from pure selfishness. The message to me was clear and simply understood. She was saying I want my life to be ok but I don't really care what happens to them. Throughout childhood and into adolescence I had imagined what I would say to her if I ever did by chance meet her, and what I had envisioned wasn't nice. So why would I want to meet that person? Simple answer "no I did not want to find Evelyn she meant absolutely nothing to me". Mom may have been cruel at times and probably was mentally ill. But at least she was still there for Clancy and me even though she would often threaten to get rid of us in one manner or another.

+However with encouragement from Carol, I agreed to attempt to locate all three of them.

My birth certificate had Charles Elmer Rickman listed as my father. However my grandmother had told me since childhood that he wasn't actually my biological father. Evelyn had started living with him sometime after he was discharged from the Navy in December of 1945. Evelyn had one child Clancy and she was 3 months pregnant with me. I also knew that she and Rickman had left Clancy and me with her parents while they went to Oklahoma to find work. It was during this time that Clancy was hit by the car. By now she had another son, my younger brother Buzzy. She told Rickman that she was going to go see Clancy to find how he was doing after the accident and bring me and him back to Oklahoma.

She left Rickman while he was at work. She left with Buzzy and all of their possessions. It was very simple to understand, for whatever the reason she and Buzzy would not be returning to Oklahoma.

She did in fact find her way to California where she immediately started living with another man and to the best of my knowledge she never returned to Oklahoma.

I started looking for Rickman first because I felt he would be the easiest to find. I also hoped he may have some knowledge of where Evelyn and possibly Buzzy may have disappeared.

I discovered that if I would send a letter to each state requesting birth records, marriage records and death certificates as well as driver's license information it was all public record.

I quickly found that Rickman still lived in Oklahoma and getting a phone # at that time was as easy as calling information. Almost every house had a phone that was listed and cell phones were not yet available.

I called Rickman and introduced myself not knowing what to expect. To my surprise he was elated that I had found him. He also had wondered what had happened to Evelyn and of the three boys. He confirmed what Rose (grandma) had said. He was indeed not my biological father; he and Evelyn had never married. He was surprised and saddened to learn that Evelyn had left us with Dad and Mom, and that Buzzy his biological son had been sold by them. He and his family came to visit us in Minnesota once; he and I stayed in touch after that occasionally exchanging phone calls until his death in 2012.

EVELYN

Evelyn was a little harder to locate. However, it wasn't as difficult as I had envisioned. Again the Department of Records in several states gave me information that led me to her. I was also able to obtain information about her life after leaving the three of us; Information that I am sure she wished I hadn't found.

When Evelyn left us with her parents that night she was with the same man she had met when she came to California to supposedly check on Clancy's health after the accident. My research revealed that Evelyn had become pregnant by a 21 year old man when she was only 14. She married that person but that marriage didn't last and they were divorced soon after they were married.

She then married Wallace La Rue. She left Wallace but did not divorce him. She then met Rickman but they never married. I was born while she was living with Rickman. They then had Rickman's child Buzzy. Evelyn left Rickman and met the man she later ran away with, Robert Bunton. She married Robert Bunton although she had never legally divorced La Rue. I decided to call her anyway if for no other reason than to find out who my biological father was. I can remember some of the conversation quite well. It went much like this,

Evelyn answered "Hello."

"Hi my name is Bud Richard Salsbury although my birth certificate says Charles Richard Rickman. Is this Evelyn Armenta Salsbury?"

Silence for a very long time. Other than the original hello these were the first words I heard my mother speak to me in 28 years.

"What do you want?"

I think I was stunned by that question for a second I'm not sure what I was expecting but I certainly hadn't prepared myself for something so cold. I almost hung up the phone. However, I had come this far so I assured her I didn't want a thing from her.

"Just tell me who my father is and I won't call you again."

Her answer was short and just as cold "it is on your birth certificate." Then she gave the phone to her husband. He knew who I was; after all he was the man in my first memory at age three the one I was running away from. He was the man who was with Evelyn the night they abandoned the three of us. These two had somehow managed to stay together for the last twenty eight years. After a period of time Evelyn came back on the line. She apologized for leaving the phone but said I had caught her off guard; she had never expected to hear from us again and she had no idea where any of us were, or that her parents had died. We talked for some time and eventually agreed that it would be good to actually meet one another. However, they weren't very affluent and could not afford a trip from Kansas to Minnesota. My wife and I weren't rich by any standard but we agreed that we would pay for them to drive to Minnesota and visit. We also made plans for Clancy and his wife Lynn to travel from Washington to Minnesota in the summer of 1977. Evelyn sent me a letter after our phone conversation which I have inserted.

Dear Zon & Family
Well I'm still in shock over the days events I'm having a terrible time convincing myself that all of you really cared enough to call me after all of these years. You'll never know the mental torment that I've been thru but in time one has to doone of two things either decide that it's over or keep on till they loose what little sanity they have then it's for sure no one wants or cares about them in most cases.

I've got a question now for you. Do you have any objections to these boys & their knowing that

152

you are my son. If so please
answer by return mail
& let me know before we
see them. We won't get
to see the younger boy for
3 yrs. as he's in Germany
but the older one pops in about
every 2 or 3 mo. for a week-end.
We know that it will not
upset them they will want
to meet & get acquainted but
want to know what your
& Clancy's feelings are s on
this.

Well there's a remote & I do
mean remote possibility that
we might can make it for
3 or 4 days the week of the 22nd.
but won't know until
the 15th to 17th for sure. Like
I told you on the phone Jim

never gone without him
except to the hospital with
one or other gus & then that
1 nite which seemed like
an eternity so hope you
will understand when I say
I just couldn't feel free to go
without my husband. You
see honey when I was real
young I know now that I was
looking for something special
& I made an awful lot of mistakes
& hurt a lot of people finding it
well I sure never intended to
hurt anybody all I did was
what I thought was best well
I know now that I was wrong
but I've had to live with that
wrong for a lot of years & believe
me it hasn't always been
easy. When you were left
with your Grandparents

I was told that I either had
to leave you or have you all
placed in Foster Homes & I sure
didn't want that. Also your
Grandmother was supposed
to have had a warrant out
for my arrest on child desertion
& as God is my witness I did
not desert you. I was young
& stupid yes to believe that all
she had to do was say the word
& you'd be taken from all of us.
I know that if I had put up a
fight Daddy would have been
caught in the middle & I can
truthfully say that I never
wanted them to have trouble
over me. Daddy sneaked to see
me several times when I lived
at Woodland also brought you to
see us but not so your
Grandmother knew it. His

the one who begged me not to cause trouble as it would have separated them & he really worshiped her. I can't explain the feelings he had for her know he was always afraid she'd leave. Now for Buppy that was over & done before I even knew they were doing it, & here again Dad begged me not to interfere well I listened for 3 reasons that prob- ably don't make sense to you but, I was real stupid about the law & a mother & her family & I was young. I'm a lot older now & I can see a lot of things that I couldn't see then & believe me I know more. You'll never know how many times I've wished I could turn the clock back but that can not be so

156

if I had been a boy she would have cared for me but as it was all she ever felt was hatred. I realize now that she had some mental problems I don't mean she was crazy I just mean she had some problems.

Well guess I'd better close & get these 2 some thing to eat. Then I'm going to write to Uncle George & see if he'll answer.

Sure want to see & get acquainted with all of you & your Family's as soon as possible.

Answer real soon
Mom Dad & Sis
Evelyn Bob Myrna Mae

Evelyn and her husband arrived in the summer of 1977 with their adopted daughter. They arrived a couple of days before my brother and his wife were to fly in from Seattle. She and I talked and she told me about her family and the two sons that her and Bob had. Both were grown with families of their own. I, in turn told her about the life Clancy and I had growing up, and of course what little I knew about Buzzy. The one thing that was puzzling to me was the fact that although she knew Rickman was not my father she stuck with that story. For Evelyn, it may have been a little unnerving that I knew so much about her past. Sunday morning I was in the shower getting ready for the day. Later that afternoon I was going to the airport to pick up Clancy and his wife. Evelyn had been excited the night before about having her sons together for the first time. Even planning a special meal to cook for that occasion. Carol came into the bathroom and told me to hurry and get out of the shower because Evelyn was leaving. What, Why, How, and When all came blundering out as I grabbed a towel a pair of pants and ran into the drive way half dressed. I was asking those same questions. I actually pleaded with her to at least wait till Clancy got there since he was flying all the way from Seattle just to see her. It fell on deaf ears. She simply replied "he wants to leave" referring to Bunton. I couldn't believe it. Carol said I was crying but I don't remember. I only knew that this was the second time in my life that she had walked out and that there would never be a third. I had to try and contact Clancy and tell him what had happened. Give him a chance to cancel his trip to Minnesota.

Although I personally never tried to contact Evelyn again I did give her address and phone number to Clancy and to Richard her younger brother who had not had contact with Evelyn since she and Bob Bunton left the three boys with her parents in 1949 or 1950. The three of them did in fact have a relationship of sorts. They would exchange occasional phone calls and they all met one time in Kansas where Evelyn lived. So even though the reunion between Evelyn and

I wasn't all that great, a mother, a son, a brother and a sister all got to see each other for the first time in 30 years. I had no contact with Evelyn after that.

I was informed of her death in 1994. I didn't know what to think but I had no feeling of regret or sadness. It was as though someone had told me of the death of a person whose name I had heard before. But that I didn't know.

Prior to her death I had forgiven her for leaving. However, I never told her that I had forgiven her or that I understood her reasons for leaving the second time. I wish now that I had. But my stubbornness, my ego and my self-preservation instincts prevented me from ever contacting her again. I wasn't going to put myself in a position to be hurt again. If we think about how often we have been forgiven it should be easy for us to forgive. But it's not. The Bible addresses this subject many times. Telling us to forgive those who wrong us just as our Heavenly Father has forgiven us.

Matt: 18: 21-22 (NIV)
Peter asked Jesus "how many times shall I forgive my brother when he sins against me seven times"?

Jesus replied "I tell you not seven times but seven times seventy".

An Interesting fact that neither Evelyn nor Rickman were aware of was that they had lived the last 30 years only about 100 miles apart. One in Kansas the other in Oklahoma. I never told either of them where the other lived. I figured it was not my place, especially since they were married to other people.

After a period of time and some soul searching, I decided to continue my search for my little brother. After all that was really what I had wanted in the first place. That and to find out who my father was.

However, after a bundle of letters sent to various state agencies and The Social Security Administration it was apparent that Lincoln Levi Rickman no longer existed.

Without some other name I could not access any information. The search for Buzzy and for my biological father had ended. I had failed.

ROAD TRIP

In the summer of 1980 I wanted to show Carol the areas where I had lived as a child. We took a very large motor home on a cross country trip going west through the southern route taking in the Grand Canyon, Disneyland and other sites as well. I showed her the orchard where my Grandfather was working the day he came in from that peach tree to proclaim that he had found Jesus. In the early 1950s the area was called Dingville, California and it still is There is a sign that even says welcome to Dingville. We then headed north to Oregon and Washington to see an old Navy friend and my brother Clancy, as well as Naches where I lived during most of my school years. I still considered Naches and Washington State my home. About 5 weeks after we had started on this cross country vacation we headed back to Minnesota on the Northern freeways. It was a great trip and we all had a wonderful time. To make the trip complete and more memorable to all of us, Carol became pregnant on that trip. There was still one more child destined to enter our family. Elizabeth our youngest, and last child, would be born in April of 1981. Our family was complete we had two sons and four daughters a good place to quit. Our quiver was full.

At the end of that vacation Carol informed me that she wouldn't mind living in a place like Washington or Oregon. She had enjoyed the scenery as well as the weather. That's all it took for me to send out resumes, ready and anxious to leave the brutal Minnesota winters.

Through my Navy training and the friends I had served with on the submarine, as well as other contacts I had made while in the Navy, I found a position in a Nuclear Power Plant on the Washington, Oregon Border. Trojan Nuclear Plant was owned and operated by Portland General Electric Company. In the summer of 1981 when Elizabeth was only 6 weeks old we were headed to Washington. All eight of us.

Our life from this point on was as normal as any family. That is if a family with 6 children can be considered normal. We argued, we fought, and did all of the other things that normal families do. I coached soccer, basketball, baseball. I still played on any team that would let me, and I also worked any overtime that was available. Eventually I even taught night classes for five years at the local college to earn extra money and dental insurance. I didn't want any of our children to feel the pain of being different because of the lack of finances in a large family. I believed that this was the price of being normal. Being part of the community something I had always wanted.

WHAT A SHOCKER

In the fall of 1992 the power plant in Oregon that I had worked in for the last 12 years sent me on a work related trip to another plant in Maine. Carol and I found a young couple willing to stay with our children that were still at home and we both went. While on that trip and listening to a radio station a news reporter informed us that the Trojan Nuclear Plant in Rainier Oregon was shutting down. I was losing my job and I found out about it on a radio station in Maine. What a shock.

In May of 1993 I actually did get laid off; and at that time we had 4 children in college. However, as strange as this may sound getting laid off was perhaps the best thing that could have happened at the time. Again God had a plan just as Jerimiah 29:11 was quoted earlier. A plan to prosper. A plan to give hope and a future.

Like most employees of my generation I always felt that the company and its retirement system would take care of me in the future. We didn't have a great deal of money in the 401K program compared to a lot of people but we had some. To us with six children any savings was a blessing. When Portland General Electric closed the plant in which I was working they sold out to a company called Enron. Within the year all of the people who had managed to stay employed had lost their 401K. Some families lost their houses and one person had to abandon the farm that had been in their family for generations. If I had stayed and continued employment with PGE I also would have lost everything. Once again I can only thank God for taking care of me and my family.

So again with my Navy contacts and training I found a position as an Electrical Maintenance Manager in a Power Plant in Tennessee working for the Tennessee Valley Authority at Watts Bar Nuclear Plant. A plant very much like the one I had just left.

The older children (the ones in college and those who were married by now) stayed in the west to continue with their lives.

Carol and our two youngest children moved to Tennessee in August of 1993. It wasn't easy moving with children in high school and Jr. High. I of all people knew how hard it is to break into a new community. However, we felt blessed to have a nice house, a steady income and I knew we would adjust to the south. It just may take a little time. However we hated being so far from the older children and the church we loved.

SURPRISE

About midnight in the fall of 1998 I received a call from a private investigator asking me if I was Bud Richard Salsbury. My heart dropped. I knew beyond doubt that one of my children was injured or had gotten onto some form of trouble either in school or in college. Why else would a private investigator call this late at night? I could only wait for the ball to drop not knowing what to expect. I told him I was indeed that person. He went on to explain that his name was Patrick Metcalf the owner of an investigative service in Texas. And if I was Bud then he was my younger brother Lincoln Levi Rickman. I think my heart stopped. I was at a loss for words but eventually I recovered and we talked forever. Pat (not Buzzy) said since he found people for a living as an investigator he thought it was only appropriate that he found his own family. Like me he was apprehensive in locating people who had given him up once before. The Metcalf's who had taken Pat as an infant had not kept it a secret that he had other relatives. But had merely said he came from a family that could not take care of him. They were both deceased so he decided to see if he could indeed find the remnants of his biological beginnings. He had located Rickman the same way I had. Rickman was still in contact with me, so he, (Rickman) provided my contact information to Pat. From there the rest was easy I had all of the information he needed to continue his search if he chose.

I told him about our family and what little I knew about his mother and two other brothers, Wally and Bobby, with the information I had gotten from Evelyn and Bunton. I also spoke of the adopted sister. Although I admit I didn't know much about her at the time and I still know very little of her now. I wasn't sure how she came to be adopted, or even if it was a legal adoption or just a placement.

We also discovered that when I went in the Navy in Nov of 1964 he dropped out of high school and joined the marines a month earlier. While I was in Navy boot camp in San Diego he was in Marine boot camp at the same place with only a chain link fence between us. He told me a story of a time when his DI (drill instructor) told his company to pick up a rock and throw it across the fence at the sailors doing drills. So I told him how we always had to hang our underwear with the fly facing the Marines symbolizing how we felt about them and our lack of respect for the Marines. We also found that each of us had married girls from the Twin Cities in Minnesota. Small world!

Pat never had the opportunity to meet or talk to Evelyn since she had died in 1994 but he did contact Bunton and found the location of the other two brothers.

They both lived in Texas only 60 miles from where he was living after retiring from the Marines. Really small world!

Pat called both Wallace and his brother Bob and made arrangements to meet them. However, one week before they were to meet Wallace died of an unexpected massive heart attack. Pat called to relay the information to me but, then again it was just a person that I had only recently heard of and not someone that I knew intimately as I would a brother.

After my meeting with Evelyn I was a little reluctant to attempt to establish a relationship with anyone from my past. As I had told

Carol repeatedly I had my family and I didn't need any one else. However, Carol firmly believed we should go to Texas and meet Pat, as well as Evelyn's remaining son Bob.

Our meeting went well. Pat and his wife Betsy and Carol and I all seemed to enjoy our time together, even though the only thing we had in common was a mother. This was also the time when I informed him of the money that transferred hands the night he was given to the Metcalf's. The Metcalf's had told him that a family was in trouble and could not take care of their children. They took him in, changed his name and went on with their lives as though he had always been theirs.

The meeting with Evelyn's son, Bob Bunton, on the other hand was awkward. Since Evelyn had died her husband Bob Sr. was living with him and his family in Texas. I was afraid of Bob Bunton Sr. when I was three, and I didn't particularly care for him when I was 31 when Evelyn came to visit 28 years after they abandon us. Strangely enough I still didn't care for him or trust him now even though I was 51. I quickly came to the conclusion that I was probably far better off being raised by my grandparents, even after all you have read, than I would have been in the house with this man.

Before we left Texas, Pat and I decided we would like to pick a time and place for the original three brothers to meet. Carol and I were living on a lake in East Tennessee at that time so we decided that everyone could come to our place for the reunion. The house was big enough and the lake provided ample opportunity for entertainment.

The three of us met there for our first time together since 1949 or 1950. It was the summer of 2001; it had been approximately 52 years since we were separated from one another behind that local bar in Winters, California. One of Clancy's first words to Pat after he was sure that he had inherited our since of humor, went something like this;

"Your kind of a slow learner aren't you?"

"Why do you say that?" Asked Pat.

"Well we sold you once but you just keep showing up".

That set the stage for the week and we had a great time.

We spent the week on the lake as well as seeing East Tennessee and enjoying the reunion. We were making up for lost time. Getting to know each other and constantly asking about our separate lives growing up. Pat's Dad was a roughneck in the oil fields. While he may not have moved quite as often as we did. He still had to move a lot and life wasn't all that easy on him either. I think everyone of us had a great time at our first reunion. That was over twenty years ago. We have seen each other separately during this time. But until recently we have not all been together. In April of 2017 we went to Pat and Betsy's home in Texas to celebrate Clancy's 75th birthday. The three of us still keep in touch. However, probably not as often as most brothers do. But then our lives weren't like most brothers.

So that's the story of "The Migrants' Child" although my life as a child may have started out a little rough, one would have to agree that it has come a long way from that little boy picking cotton at age 5 and living in one room shacks at the edge of the fields. Always moving to follow whatever crop was in season, picking whatever was ready to harvest at the time. My hope in writing this, is that each person who reads it comes away with the message that no matter the circumstances, no matter how hard we try to turn our back on God. He won't turn his back on us. God's grace is always available to us. It is ours for the asking. The phrase "around the clock 24/7" will always apply to the God I love and who loves me. We only need to ask. It is a gift! It is free and it cannot be taken away by anyone.

APPENDIX

Before I put the finishing touches on this writing Carol and others have suggested that I include some things about my career and the positions that I held as I have worked my way toward retirement. It's not that I was anything great like a corporate executive. But I guess my career has been unusual for a person with no more education than mine, to have attained positions of leadership that I have attained within the work force. It also makes the Grace and abundance of God's Grace in my life real.

As I stated earlier I started my career after the Navy as an Instrument Technician in a fossil power plant in Minnesota. During the interview I asked a couple of questions about the chemistry of the plant. I was asked if I understood the chemistry and was hired. Then put in the position responsible for the water quality for the plant. I was told with my Navy training and experience my beginning salary would be between $4.00 and $4.50 per hour. True to their word I started at $4.02. I managed to keep my head above water and eventually took the test to be one of the 1st people in the company to obtain the position of Sr. Instrument Technician. This was a new position created within the company for those who had completed all the other requirements within their job and it gave us a place and salary above those who had not yet been recommended for the position.

Shortly after reaching that goal I left Northern States Power and went to work in Trojan Nuclear Plant for Portland General Electric Co. (PGE). I was a senior Instrument Technician at this plant and at one point even became the union steward representing the Instrument Techs. Several times the maintenance manager asked if I would accept a position in management but I always refused. Primarily due to financial incentives. I was told that I had the leadership skills to manage people, but I couldn't see it. I know that all through my school years I had been in positions of leadership. I was student body president, a quarterback, the point guard in basketball and had coached and managed in every sport I ever played. But this was different it wasn't a game.

I finally agreed to a position as the Metrology Manager at Trojan in the spring of 1992. In the fall I heard about the plant closure as I detailed earlier, and in the spring of 1993 I was laid off and eventually accepted the position in Tennessee. This is important because had I not accepted the management position I would have still been in the union and as such would have been protected from a layoff due to my seniority. Remember all those people that lost everything? I would have been one of them.

In Tennessee I came in as a manager the job was good but the hours were awful. There were times I would be up all night at work and after only a couple of hours sleep get called back. Trying to start up a plant is hard work and demands long hours. I was averaging 3500 hours per year and being compensated for 2080 hours. One morning after being up all night the plant manager called and ask to speak with me. Carol said no. I had just gone to bed and she wasn't going to disturb me. He insisted but she can be pretty stubborn. The next day I heard about it. From both him and from her. He was saying I needed to educate my wife. And she was saying you need to find another job this one is going to kill you.

I did indeed find another job in 1999. A position requiring fewer hours and was far less traumatic than trying to educate my wife.

Our country along with other NATO countries entered a treaty to rid the world of certain Weapons of Mass Destruction (WMD). TVA is a government agency that has been working with the army in the explosive materials field since before WWII. They had been supplying people and expertise to the Army for the last several years in the effort to develop ways to destroy WMDs.

The TVA act in part states that TVA is to support National Defense in various ways and means as requested. I applied to work with this branch of TVA and was accepted. Probably as much because I volunteered as it was my qualifications. TVA at that time had individuals at various weapons storage sites across the country as well as a few in overseas areas. This branch had approximately 200 individuals doing a variety of assignments. There were Project Managers, Chemist, Engineers, Union Labor Trades and me. I was still employed by TVA but I was on loan to the Army so I took all of my direction from them. The only contact I had with TVA was my check every two weeks. I loved this arrangement. The project I was selected for was in a little known place named Dugway, Utah. Dugway is an army base in the middle of nowhere. I was going to be overseeing a research project to develop a technology for the destruction of weapons of mass destruction. I had no idea what that meant or how it related to the operation of a power plant but it was further west than Tennessee and the hours were better.

I often told people when questioned about where Dugway was. That if you want to get to Dugway you simply must take interstate 80 approximately 40 miles west of Salt Lake City to the middle of nowhere. Then take exit 77 and go another 40 miles south through open range grazing and to the end of the earth. At that point you will have arrived at Dugway. Here the pavement ended and the old

Pony Express Trail would take you through the desert to Nevada and beyond.

Carol and I lived on the Army base. We were allowed to use all of the facilities because of the long distance to Salt Lake. To some this would be a horrible assignment but we absolutely loved it. We would take the car into the desert on weekends and after work finding various rocks and gemstones as well as the herd of wild horses that called this piece of deserted desert their home. The horses were amazing and so beautiful to watch. I had access to the base rock shop and we spent hours cutting and polishing the rocks and stones we found on our excursions to the surrounding desert. To us this was God's creation and we enjoyed our time exploring it. Occasionally we would drive the almost 100 miles to Salt Lake for dinner or shopping or even to take advantage of the Mormon Genealogical Library. We could spend hours trying to discover anything at all about our families. It was fun and a very inexpensive date.

My adult supervision as I referred to them were at Aberdeen Proving Grounds (APG) in Maryland. Two individuals that I have become very fond of and over the years we have become friends. We have a relationship far different than just co-workers or supervisors. They would visit the site about every 3-4 weeks and as they grew more comfortable with my ability the visits became less frequent. We had daily conference calls and I was to keep them informed of the progress of the project. Sounded simple enough but the best part of all, was that I had no people to supervise. It didn't take long before I realized I enjoyed the people I was working for as much as I did the job. However, I also realized very quickly that the technology they were pursuing was headed nowhere. I had to tell them my opinion knowing that I could possibly lose this great assignment. To keep it to myself and just ride it out like others were doing would have been wrong. I chose to step forward and let them know they were wasting money and time; only to find that they had made that same decision earlier. They were waiting to see if a new pair of eyes would see the same things they had. The crew was great, but the technology we were using would not work for our application. It took 18 months after my report but the job funding was eventually pulled. Instead of laying me off my adult leadership wanted me to take another project. This time it was the Explosive Destruction System (EDS). Carol and I would be moving to Livermore, California and working with Sandia National Labs. I was going to be overseeing the construction, design and development of a second generation of EDS's. This one bigger and more complicated than the first one that was already in service. It's a good thing Carol was flexible and enjoyed seeing different parts of the country. She agreed to the move and that she was with me for the ride. While at Sandia I believe I worked with some of the most intelligent people our nation has to offer in this field. As a Government Representative I didn't really direct their work but my suggestions were considered the same as if it had come from headquarters. I still didn't have to supervise people.

Several times over the years I was asked what I did at Sandia. I had a standard response. I explained that Sandia was like a village of extremely intelligent people and like all villages it needs a village idiot. That's my job. I bring common sense to confusion.

Sandia completed the EDS on time and within budget. This was considered unusual for our typical Government contracts. I believe it was because of Sandia's dedication to the project and in a small way my presence as a representative of the army. My presence meant they no longer had to wait for answers from back east which was often compounded by the difficulty of a three hour time difference between the east and the west coast. See what I mean common sense to confusion.

We finished design and construction in the winter of 2001 and our next hurdle would be finding a place to test this beast. The United

States has a lot of chemical warfare in storage bunkers at various locations in several states. However, getting past the environmental regulations can take years. Everyone wanted the EDS tested as soon as possible. However, the common complaint was that it wasn't licensed. Therefore, it can't be tested in our state. Kind of a "catch 22". We needed to test to be able to get the license but we couldn't test because we didn't have a license.

We all knew there were plenty of Chemical Warfare Munitions in Europe as well as other countries. But it would be difficult to convince the Army to spend the money required for overseas testing on an untested system. I kept encouraging my supervisor for a test anywhere in Europe. But then I had nothing to say about it, I just liked to push on my adult leadership when I could. Besides I had never been to Europe.

As my supervisor often said "no good deed goes unpunished". I was called to Maryland in November and told that we would indeed be testing in the UK. I was to return to California and assist in packing up the EDS (about 57000 lbs.) and ready it for shipment to the UK.

On the way back to Sandia I tried to come up with a good way to surprise Carol with this news. Although we had entertained the idea of going to Europe neither of us thought it would ever happen. However, even if it were to happen why would I get to go?

I came through the door to the house that we were renting in Tracy, California, and Carol as she so often does took one look at me and said what's up. I replied nothing just tired from the trip. Her response was "don't give me that, you've got that look what's going on?" I informed her that "we are going to test the EDS in England". "Right" she said "now tell me what is going on". It took several minutes for me to convince her but eventually she believed me. Now for the hard part. I had to convince her that we were going to test

174

in Salisbury England. However, to convince her that I was serious and not just fooling around took considerably longer this time. It did finally sink in and we were both ecstatic for different reasons. I saw dollar signs floating around with overseas pay and tax free income and per diem. She, on the other hand saw travel brochures and airline tickets with a chance to spend time seeing Europe. We sat down and discussed our differences in expectations and came to a mutual conclusion. Hers! We would not save a penny but we were going to see as much of Europe as we could squeeze into my work schedule. True to our mutual agreement we traveled a lot and enjoyed every trip we could take.

We landed in London in a rain and snow storm after being up all night on the flight over. I picked up the car and we were off; on the wrong side of the road, the wrong side of the car and roundabouts everywhere. We drove through the airport 3 times before I finally got the exit figured out and found the correct road to Salisbury.

We lived in Porton, a village just outside of the town of Salisbury on the Salisbury Plain about 10 minutes from Stonehenge. I went to the gate to get a pass on my first day and the lady in the office commented with a very strong accent "your name is Salsbury"; "yes". "Well you don't spell your name quite proper you know". I responded with "well it works quite well in America. In America we felt why put a letter in you don't need? Therefore, the letter I has been taken out and it works just fine".

They also had one other comment that I found amusing. When we informed them that we would like to bring the EDS to the UK and would require their weapons for us to use during testing. I think the conversation was something like this; "let me see if I have this straight. You want to come to the UK and destroy our bombs and you will pay us to do that. Our response "Yes but we will require quite a few of them for our test." "You yanks are so crazy, how many bombs would you require we have thousands of them you know".

My assignment was to act as the Government Liaison between all of the different groups that were there. Some were there to observe, some to do maintenance while others were to operate the unit for the first time.

At the end of the project Carol and I had been able to fit visiting 17 different countries into my schedule. No money in the saving account but what an experience we had. It's amazing that the same God that made America so beautiful made Europe as well. It is also a beautiful place.

My supervisors at APG had to budget for my hours each year because after all I was still employed by TVA but on loan to the DoD and the Army. To do this at my salary required a title so I became an Engineer without a degree of any kind. Not having attended college I argued the point with them that I was not an engineer and that I had never driven a train either. But in the end I was listed by them as a senior engineer. A non-degreed engineer.

We finished the testing in England again on time and within budget. Something that a lot of government projects have not been able to do.

Again "No good deed goes unpunished" we wanted a bigger unit one that was faster and could destroy more items at a time, it needed to be more versatile and they wanted it in a year. My job was back in California at Sandia National Labs one more time. Carol and I rented an apartment in Livermore, California, and were only there 3 months when I was called back to Maryland. For a meeting. It seemed as though the supervisors of my adult supervisions and TVA wanted more of my presence in Maryland. During all of the time that Carol and I were traveling for the Army, DoD and TVA we still had a house in Tennessee on Watts Bar Lake just outside of Knoxville. Anytime I had a break or time off we would go there. But they wanted me at our office in Maryland when I wasn't traveling. An office that had about 20 TVA employees supporting various Army projects. One of those employees was my son Jamie a mechanical engineer.

The idea was to sell the place in Tennessee. And establish a home in Maryland close to Aberdeen. The good news was that our youngest son Jamie and his family had gone to work for the same group of TVA and was working for the Army in Maryland just as I was. I knew that I would only be in the office on rare occasions when I wasn't in the field supervising a research project. Which, by the way, was where I felt I belonged not in some office behind a desk.

Selling the lake house was not that hard. Jamie and his family and Carol and I decided to buy a house together and we settled on a house that was big enough for an in-law suite or a place Carol and I could sleep when we were in town. Jamie's family was satisfied with the house and the neighborhood. I think Jamie and Erica (his wife) picked it out and we all agreed.

This is part of my work story that I always enjoyed reliving only because it was so unusual even for me. We closed on the house at 10:00 am, then went to lunch. I was back in the office at 1:00 pm and was called to the conference room. Two TVA supervisors who were also good friends informed me that I needed to be in Newport, Indiana as quick as possible, no later than two weeks from today. I was being transferred from my work in California with Sandia to supervise a crew of TVA employees in Indiana. I had owned the house I had just closed on for 3 hours. Of course I said no I'm not going. We argued for some time about whether or not I would go but I stuck to my guns and continued to refuse. They talked money and position and I talked reality. I was just not going to do this. I knew the project there was falling down around TVA's ears and if I stepped in at this point I would bear the blame for the failure of the project. Rather than those who had put it into that position to begin with.

I was also aware that if it were to turn out successful those ahead of me would claim the credit for that success. Stating that they were already on the road to recovery. And that I merely took over a successful program. I just wasn't going to Indiana. To give you an idea of what it was like, a TVA engineer whom I grew to have great respect for; wrote a report for the Army stating "the problems at this site are so blatant that even Ray Charles could see them". That statement almost cost her a career. But it was accurate as well as funny. However, the final argument that convinced me to change my mind and accept this position was the senior managers' statement that the Army was going to dismiss all TVA employees working on all Army projects if we couldn't turn this particular rat's nest into a positive outcome. That would require getting it within the budget and time constraints that had originally been predicted by TVA 3 years previously. The next statement they made was blunt and directly to the point. But it gave me the incentive to do whatever I needed to make this work. If you fail, all 200 people in this division working for the Army would lose their jobs. Personally I only cared about 2 of them; my son and myself. I accepted the assignment. I had never managed a project with a $250 million dollar budget before. Or a project where the livelihood of others was placed on my shoulders. No pressure on this job.

I can only assume that their selection of me was because of the successful completion of the last projects and that TVA was running out of options. My biggest concern and disappointment was that I would be reporting to TVA rather than to the Army. I was not at all happy about any of this. Least of all telling Carol we were leaving so soon.

I called Carol to relay the bad news. I think I said something like "Carol don't unpack we are headed to Indiana". I remember her response. "Oh good that's like going back to the Midwest, it will be fun". And so we went. I never shared my incentive for going with anyone but her.

I took the assignment knowing full well that it would be difficult. I felt like the analogy of bacon and eggs. The chicken that supplies the eggs is involved in the meal. But the pig that supplies the bacon is committed. I was committed; and there was no turning around at this point.

An instructor once told me that if a company has problems ask the workers on the floor how to fix them, and listen to their solutions. They are intimate with the issues. It was good advice.

The Colonel and the civilian department head for the Army projects called me to their office and asked what I was going to do and what made me think I could change the outcome. We spoke for a while and I outlined what I intended to implement. They agreed and decided to give the program 6 months to show positive improvement or everyone would go home and a civilian contracting company would step in to take over. Again no pressure!

The site in Newport Indiana had been used to produce a nerve agent VX in the 1960s. VX is an organophosphate that is a tasteless, odorless, and liquid, with an amber color. It has an extremely high boiling point and the consistency of motor oil. It takes less than a drop to kill. Fortunately we never used it in war. However, since we had entered that treaty with other NATO countries to destroy our stockpile of certain Weapons of Mass Destruction as well as the facilities that produced them. Our job was to dismantle and destroy this facility that was used during that production period. All of the pipes, tanks pumps heaters and in some cases even the walls were contaminated with VX. To the best of my knowledge this was the first time this had been attempted.

I won't bore you with the details of all that happened but the project was 18 months behind schedule. It was scheduled to be completed in a little under 3 years. That meant we had to do 4-1/2 years of work in a 3 year period. I called the crew together on the first day and explained who I was and what my function would be. Some of the people in that room still remark about that speech. Therefore, it must have made an impression on some of them. I didn't care. I didn't ask for the job and there was very little chance for success. After that day the majority of the crew opted to follow my leadership. They were happy to give solutions to problems that had been holding them back. And they were willing to be resourceful as well as innovative in the approach to save time and money. However, unfortunately there were those who chose to leave, while others were asked to leave. The ones who stayed with the project worked hard, came up with innovative ideas for improvement and we completed the project in a little over 2 years almost 8 months ahead of the predicted schedule. A feat that no one thought possible. During that two year time frame I worked 6 days per week and about 14-16 hours per day. When I took over the project there were approximately 150 people at the site. Probably 75 TVA employees and 75 contractors of various unions and disciplines. All of them from the Tennessee Valley area, "The Valley" as it was referred to by those working for TVA.

To better understand some of the issues I dealt with let me relay a couple of stories that were humorous to me, however serious to those individuals involved.

At one point, I had an individual complain about a person in his car pool that had a cat with fleas. Because of this cat he now had fleas, and his apartment had fleas. He was requesting that I have his car and apartment fumigated.

Another individual complained that someone in his carpool would fart and then lock all of the windows. I later found that one of the people in that car opened the door and the driver continued driving for the next 45 miles at 65 MPH, with the door open in a Government vehicle. I called the guilty parties into my office with their foremen and union stewards. I then stepped out and said I'll be back in 5 minutes and that's all the time you have to tell me why I shouldn't send both of these individuals home immediately. I was promised they would never bother me with this kind of garbage again and they didn't. On one occasion I had a person ask if it was ok to display his degrees on the wall. I asked if it would make him a better supervisor. (He had two Masters Degrees). We discussed that idea for a few minutes then I informed him that when he saw me put all of my degrees on the wall he could follow suit. That night I asked Carol if I should ever tell the people that I only possessed a high school diploma and was barely able to get that. We decided to keep it between us. The chemist at the site would often show me a chemical solution to a problem and never once did I let them know I had little or no idea what they had just shown me. My job was to surround myself with people who were knowledgeable and then empower and trust their abilities. It worked well.

During my time at Newport I was called to the Pentagon for briefings twice. The first time I was told what to wear and what to say. When I arrived I was greeted by a member of the staff who knew way more about me than I had envisioned. Needless to say I was more than a little nervous. The second time I was briefed the day before by the Colonel and our civilian director. We had discovered a small tank full of pure VX. The crew responded just as they were trained and had it destroyed immediately. This tank was not supposed to be there and did not show on any of the drawings we possessed. The Army wanted to talk about how we found it, destroyed it, and stored the byproducts. No one was going to speak except the Director. The rest of us were there for moral support and to answer any questions that may come up that he did not have an immediate answers for. We were briefing the Deputy Secretary of the Army plus a room full of other government officials. This was a good plan I just needed to sit there and say nothing. After the second or third question the director looked at me and said "let's ask Bud he was there and he is in charge of the site". Fortunately I was there and I had the answers to their questions.

The crew at Newport that dismantled that facility have every right to be proud of themselves for the work they did. They did all the work; I only gave them the support they needed to do it. After the first 6 months I was convinced that they could do it. They could clean up this site on time and under budget. It was a difficult job. A job that no one had ever done before. One that could cost you your life if you made a mistake.

Some of the TVA managers seemed upset by our success. It seemed as though the site was always under scrutiny by someone. We often were accused of taking shortcuts or ignoring safety rules, but no one ever found a single thing that they could say we were doing wrong. We weren't taking shortcuts or sacrificing safety for the sake of schedule, we merely became a team, and I was the coach. A coach's job is to get his players to perform better than they think they can. A manager's job is to get the workers to produce more than they think they can. A manager is nothing more than a coach, and coaching was something I did understand.

When we finished the project I was told that we were about $40 million dollars under our predicted budget. Partly because we had finished early. But we finished early because the crew was constantly coming up with new ideas for ways to handle the difficult situations we faced. I told the Army I wasn't greedy and would accept a mere 5% bonus. But it fell on deaf ears. Imagine that!!

A lot of people have given credit to me for this success. However I feel differently. I have a strong belief that God gave me the talent to lead and then put me where I could use the talent he gave me. Those people who were in the field deserve the credit for the work that was done. They took all of the risks involved. My only involvement was to remove the roadblocks preventing them from doing the job and being successful.

When we were done in Indiana I was told again "No good deed goes unpunished." "How would you like to go back to Utah?"

UTAH

I would again be working with TVA personnel on a project to dismantle another facility. This one used to test the various chemical agents used for war.

I really wanted to go back to working on the research side of the projects and I wanted to work for my adult leadership at APG not for TVA. However, I was told that if I would at least get this project started I could return to Sandia as soon as the army started the design of the next generation of the EDS.

Carol and I moved to Tooele Utah. Tooele is a bedroom community about 25 miles from Salt Lake City and about 50 60 miles from Dugway where Carol and I lived when I first started working with the Army. We purchased a house in Tooele and began to enjoy the community. I was fortunate to have a majority of the people that had been working with me in Indiana comprise the crew to dismantle this facility. Some of those same people that had hated me when I came to Newport were now considered friends. These people from The Valley were willing to follow me to the desert of Utah and take on the task of destroying another bunch of buildings and all of the secrets that they held. I was humbled by this.

On the weekends I showed some of those from Alabama and Tennessee the Utah that Carol and I had learned to love when we lived in Dugway in 1999. They saw the rocks, the desert, the wild horses, the mountains behind Salt Lake City, and the beauty of the high mountain lakes. We also went snowmobiling in Yellowstone National Park; seeing and doing things that this group had never experienced. I still get phone calls and messages from those who went on that trip requesting that if I would arrange another snowmobiling trip to Yellowstone, they would fly out to Salt Lake City so we could all go on another winter trip to one of my favorite places. Yellowstone in the winter is a magical place.

In 2010 TVA decided that they no longer wanted to be involved with any Army Projects that required their employees to work outside of the TVA area (The Valley as it was referred to). That meant that everyone would have to come back and either work in the valley or not at all.

In 2005 TVA had sent out a notice requesting my anticipated retirement date so they could hire and train my replacement. At that time I flippantly responded with 10/10 /10

With the option of going back to Tennessee and working for the TVA managers as my only choice. I chose the not at all option. I retired from TVA on October 10 2010 or 10/10/10 just as I had told them in 2005.

Twelve hours after my retirement from TVA, my adult leadership in Aberdeen called and asked me to come to work. I was going to be working as a contractor for the Army. Going wherever they felt I was needed the most. I often traveled to cities where some part or piece of the EDS or other technologies were being made or tested. Again I loved my job and the fact that I didn't have to supervise anyone made it even better.

I continued in this role as a contractor until Sept. 30, 2016 when I retired a second time. My wife and I now live in a small town in Idaho close to two of our children and some of our grandchildren. We spend the winters traveling like so many others our age trying to stay active, involved in life and avoid the cold weather.

Maybe this time I will stay retired; who knows. But for now; life is good and God's Grace is still abundant in my life. Each day I can ask "Why Me" "what did I do to deserve so many blessings".

EPILOGUE

When I started writing this story I did not intend for it to be a Spiritual or Christian writing. I was simply going to write the story of my childhood for my children and my grandchildren. However, as I wrote I realized that my childhood and these stories are not just about me. They are more about a God that has been so gracious and faithful in my life that I can't just write him out and not include him in these stories. During all of the events in my life God has been there. I will not apologize to anyone for making that known. Hopefully, those who read this will think about the times in their lives that are unexplainable. Each of us have had those experiences. All too often those times are just written off as luck. You survive a crash, and someone says you were lucky, or perhaps during war you walk away from battle while others fall. If you write it all off as just luck or the alignment of the universe. Then a baby's first breath would also be; just luck. It would be luck that the stars don't fall on us at night. Or that the sun still shines and gives us warmth during the day.

I personally believe that there is a God; A God that; loves us unconditionally; One that cries every time we say "wow I was lucky", instead of "Thank you God for getting me through yet another day". I am also very grateful to those who had a part in impacting my life. I don't believe I would have been where I am today were it not for those individuals.

My grandparents who took me in when they really didn't have to; and couldn't afford it. After reading this story you are aware of the hard time I had with them. However, my grandfather had a huge impact on my life. His prayers for me were answered and I appreciate all he taught me growing up. There were others such as Jim Cullen and his wife that believed in me; and gave me a chance to experience a normal family. They even went so far as to introduce me to my wife who has stood beside me and prayed for me for 50 years. There were some teachers and coaches that believed if I were given the opportunity and held accountable at some level, I could not only do the scholastic requirements but I could excel in them as well. My supervisors from the Army and a few at TVA that saw the leadership abilities that God had given me; and gave me the opportunity to use it. And of course my wife who has been there through so many hard times and yet still has faith in me. Her example has had a great influence in my search for Christianity. Without her I would not be who I am today. The message is that no one can do it alone and I certainly didn't either. As I said previously I'm not a super star or a CEO but I have accomplished a lot more than was expected by most. I thank God for the people he has put in my life and the difference each has made.

I have only told of God's hand and his Grace involving Kim and Amy. But the other 4 children have stories of their own as well. Stories that as they walked away they should have been saying the same thing I have said repeatedly during this story. "There are some things that only God can get you through". These stories are certainly not all inclusive. There are others that I could have been mentioned and probably some they would rather I didn't know about.

I am so thankful that God was with them during these times.

Brad

Go back to a night when you were in high school and decided to show the kids from a neighboring school how well you could hold your liquor.

That night you almost died of alcohol poisoning. When a Dr. who just happened to be on that particular road found you unconscious lying beside your still running car you were almost dead.

What are the odds that on that particular night a Dr. that loved to look at stars would have come back down out of the hills at that very time when you needed help the most? Just like the car wreck I walked away from son; sometimes in life there are things that only God can get you through. Those things are sometimes unexplainable. But God wasn't done with you yet.

James

I remember when a friend of ours lost his life while duck hunting on the Columbia River. Speculation is that his boat capsized and the gear worn while hunting weighted him down. He was an experienced hunter and boats-man but the water was cold and swift.

How long after that was it that you and a friend also capsized? In about the same area. You lost the guns, all of the material things in the boat but somehow you were able to stay afloat and work your way to some abandon pilings. Pilings that were underwater. You couldn't see them and yet you found them. By all standards you shouldn't have had a chance of survival. Think about it this way. Two boys who were ill-equipped to be in the water under those conditions, and yet somehow manage to ignore the extremely cold temperature or the weight of the clothes worn to hunt ducks. You both manage to climb out by yourselves with no help; I don't think so. You had the hand of God guiding you out of that river and on to the shore. The odds are too great to be anything else.

Cherie

You were born in Da Nang a city in communist controlled North Viet Nam. How you managed to escape to South Viet Nam is certainly a feat that God had to have orchestrated. You left South Viet Nam just as it was coming apart; you were on one of the last planes to remove children from a war torn country. After Viet Nam fell children who were orphans, children of Amer–Asian decent and those families that had any contact with the US agencies operating in that country were killed. In all likelihood, had you not been on that plane, you would probably have been one of those children. By God's Grace you were spared and came to live with us. The same pediatrician that had seen Kim when we took her from the airport to the hospital saw you also, and said you were perhaps the healthiest young lady he had seen coming out of Viet Nam. Twice your life was spared before you were even two years old. What a miracle and blessing you were.

Liz

When you were into your teenage and college years I recall quite vividly your adventures kayaking and rafting on various rivers. If we were to go back in time you could easily recall a kayak that was held underwater for probably 20 minutes but you somehow freed yourself from the boat and was forced to the surface. The Hydraulics that held the kayak underwater could have easily held you there just as well, but it didn't.

On the Colorado River I remember a time when a newly trained oarsmen capsized your raft and pinned you against a rock holding you underwater. Somehow you managed to find the strength to pull yourself up the face of the rock and to the surface. There were other times as well but you get the idea. God was there when you needed him.

As a veteran I was given the option to have a headstone in the Idaho State Veterans Cemetery. Mine is simple. It's something I want to be remembered by, and one of my favorite things to tell others. And a good place to end this story.

"God has a plan for your life-"just listen".

The End

THE MIGRANTS' CHILD

I hope you have enjoyed reading about The Migrants' Child. But most of all I hope you received the messages that I wish to convey.

Don't let anyone separate you from God regardless of how wrong you may think they are. In the end you are the only one that will suffer.

God does have a plan for your life –"please listen"

Bud

Clancy and I in Chicago 1954

Dad and Mom in Naches 1956

Me, Dad, Mom and Clancy A Typical Sunday in 1956

Me in Imperial 1963

Printed in Poland
by Amazon Fulfillment
Poland Sp. z o.o., Wrocław